D0744662

ALBERTA
WAYSIDE
WILDFLOWERS

Linda Kershaw

LONE
PINE

Lone Pine Publishing

The Publisher: Lone Pine Publishing

10145 – 81 Avenue

Edmonton, AB, Canada T6E 1W9

1808 – B Street NW, Suite 140

Auburn, WA, USA 98001

Website: www.lonepinepublishing.com

National Library of Canada Cataloguing in Publication Data

Kershaw, Linda J., 1951–
 Alberta wayside wildflowers / Linda Kershaw.

 Includes bibliographical references and index.
 ISBN 1-55105-350-0

 1. Wild flowers—Alberta—Identification. I. Title.
QK203.A4K47 2003   582.13'097123   C2002-910726-1

Editorial Director: Nancy Foulds
Project Editor: Dawn Loewen
Illustrations Coordinator: Carol Woo
Production Coordinator: Jennifer Fafard
Book Design: Heather Markham
Layout & Production: Heather Markham, Lynett McKell
Cover Design: Gerry Dotto
Botanical Illustrations: Linda Kershaw
Scanning, Separations & Film: Elite Lithographers Co.

All interior photos by Linda Kershaw except the following, reproduced with the kind permission of their copyright holders: Lorna Allen, 37b, 40a, 100b, 125a, 135b; Terry Clayton, 63a, 90a&b, 114a, 126b, 135a, 143a&b; Robert Frisch, 120a

DISCLAIMER: This guide is not meant to be a 'how-to' reference for using plants. We do not recommend experimentation by readers, and we caution that many plants, including some traditional medicines, are poisonous or otherwise harmful. Self-medication with herbs is unwise, and wild plant foods should be used with caution and with expert advice.

We acknowledge the financial support of the Government of Canada through the Book Publishing Industry Development Program (BPIDP) for our publishing activities.

PC: P1

Contents

The wildflowers in this guide, arranged by flower colour

strawberry-blite
p. 63

common red paintbrush
p. 39

wood lily
p. 113

scarlet globe-mallow
p. 138

great blanketflower
p. 75

prairie coneflower
p. 76

greater bladderwort
p. 40

yellow lady's-slipper
p. 36

common tansy
p. 88

bird's-foot-trefoil
p. 53

annual sunflower
p. 74

marsh ragwort
p. 86

Canada goldenrod
p. 93

perennial sow-thistle
p. 70

common dandelion
p. 71

hairy false-golden-aster
p. 77

spike-like goldenrod
p. 92

yellow pond-lily
p. 115

yellow mountain-avens
p. 129

meadow buttercup
p. 117

common silverweed
p. 130

graceful cinquefoil
p. 133

sweet-clover
p. 56

yellow watercrowfoot
p. 118

fringed gromwell
p. 143

curly-cup gumweed
p. 78

narrow-leaved
hawkweed, p. 69

annual hawk's-beard
p. 68

butter-and-eggs
p. 38

fringed yellow-
loosestrife, p. 124

yellow marsh-marigold
p. 116

shrubby cinquefoil
p. 131

plains cinquefoil
p. 132

golden-bean
p. 52

yellow avens
p. 127

wormseed wallflower
p. 105

tumbleweed mustard
p. 106

great mullein
p. 141

pale false-dandelion
p. 72

common goat's-beard
p. 73

heart-leaved Alexanders
p. 95

common evening-
primrose, p. 140

wild mustard
p. 107

prickly-pear cactus
p. 114

golden corydalis
p. 37

leafy spurge
p. 94

pineappleweed
p. 89

American licorice
p. 54

American milk-vetch
p. 51

northern bedstraw
p. 103

curly dock
p. 104

starry false-
Solomon's-seal, p. 111

northern grass-of-
Parnassus, p. 121

cream-coloured
vetchling, p. 50

water calla
p. 61

common cow-parsnip
p. 96

buck-bean
p. 108

common yarrow
p. 91

Canada anemone
p. 119

Virginia strawberry
p. 128

arctic sweet-colt's-foot
p. 87

arum-leaved arrowhead
p. 109

field mouse-ear-
chickweed, p. 122

false-toadflax
p. 99

oxeye daisy
p. 79

scentless chamomile
p. 80

rusty Labrador-tea
p. 135

Canada violet
p. 45

spotted water-hemlock
p. 98

white death-camas
p. 112

common water-parsnip
p. 97

bunchberry
p. 62

field bindweed
p. 147

smooth fleabane
p. 84

brittle-stem hemp-nettle
p. 43

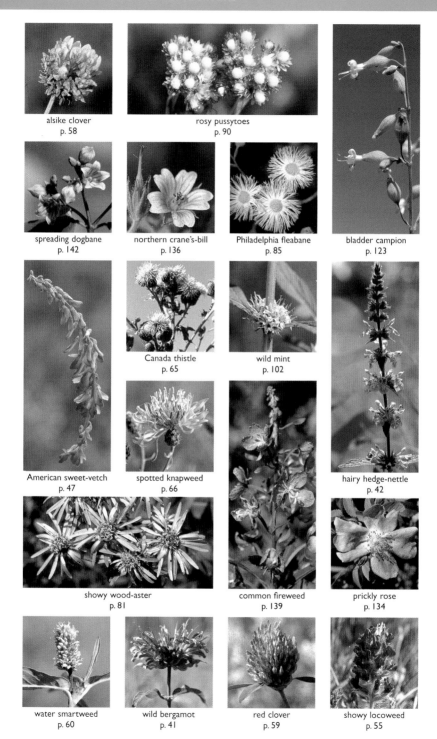

alsike clover
p. 58

rosy pussytoes
p. 90

bladder campion
p. 123

spreading dogbane
p. 142

northern crane's-bill
p. 136

Philadelphia fleabane
p. 85

American sweet-vetch
p. 47

Canada thistle
p. 65

wild mint
p. 102

hairy hedge-nettle
p. 42

spotted knapweed
p. 66

showy wood-aster
p. 81

common fireweed
p. 139

prickly rose
p. 134

water smartweed
p. 60

wild bergamot
p. 41

red clover
p. 59

showy locoweed
p. 55

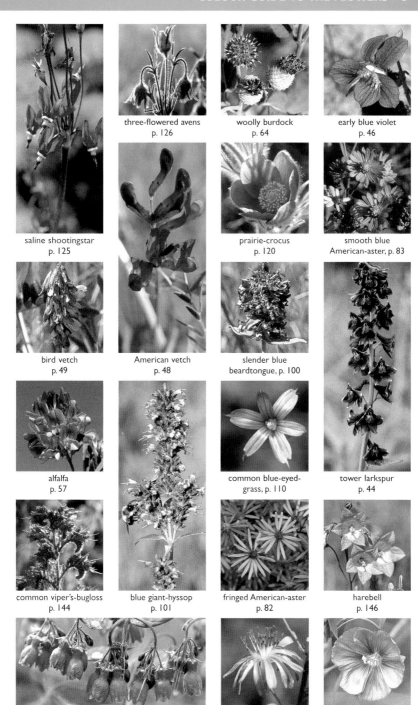

saline shootingstar
p. 125

three-flowered avens
p. 126

woolly burdock
p. 64

early blue violet
p. 46

prairie-crocus
p. 120

smooth blue
American-aster, p. 83

bird vetch
p. 49

American vetch
p. 48

slender blue
beardtongue, p. 100

alfalfa
p. 57

common blue-eyed-
grass, p. 110

tower larkspur
p. 44

common viper's-bugloss
p. 144

blue giant-hyssop
p. 101

fringed American-aster
p. 82

harebell
p. 146

tall bluebells
p. 145

common blue lettuce
p. 67

wild blue flax
p. 137

Why Learn More About Wildflowers?

Imagine a summer without wildflowers: an endless monotony of brown, grey and green. Instead of that boring scene, our eyes are treated to yellows, oranges, pinks, whites and purples, a colourful patchwork that changes throughout the summer. Wildflowers add beauty and variety to the roads, streets, sidewalks and pathways that crisscross our countryside.

But wayside wildflowers provide much more than simple decoration. Many of these hardy plants are important to the ecology of disturbed areas such as roadsides and vacant lots. At first, newly cleared areas are simply bare soil, usually with lots of rocks, low fertility and a tendency to wash away in the rain. Only the toughest plants can tolerate such harsh conditions. Those that do survive help make the soil more fertile for other plants and help hold the soil so it isn't swept away by wind and water. Common wildflowers also provide food and shelter for lots of different animals.

Many wildflowers have fascinating histories that extend back for centuries. Local Native peoples used many of these plants for food and medicine long before settlers arrived from Europe. Almost one-quarter of the plants in this guide, however, were brought to North America from Europe and Asia. Some

common fireweed

arrived as valued garden plants, but others sneaked in with livestock and crop seed. Nowadays, some of the species in this guide are considered weeds—unwanted but highly successful plants that can choke out crops and gardens (see p. 14). Yet, to a casual passerby, they remain beautiful wildflowers, blanketing waysides with a mosaic of colours and textures.

It's fun to get to know wildflowers by name. Just as recognizing your friends Judy, Roy, Bill and Inger means much more than seeing a group of strangers, recognizing prickly rose, common fireweed, bird's-foot-trefoil and bunchberry means more than simply seeing 'some plants.' Once you know what to look for, it's easy to see the differences between wildflowers and to learn their names. Getting to know common flowers gives us a glimpse of the great variety of life around us, even in roadside ditches.

What Is a Wildflower?

Most of us enjoy all sorts of flowers through the year and recognize many different types, from tulips in our gardens, to carnations at the florist's, to dandelions growing wild. But what exactly is a flower, and why do plants produce such an amazing array of showy, colourful blooms?

The main function of a flower is to produce seed so that the plant can leave offspring, spread to new areas and increase in number. Technically, a flower is a shortened shoot with a compact cluster of leaves that have been modified into specialized structures (such as petals) for reproduction. Most of the wildflowers in this guide have *perfect* flowers, with both male and female parts, but some species have male flowers on one plant and female flowers on another. The illustration on this page shows a cross-section of a typical perfect flower.

Let's start with the most important parts: the male and female structures.

The male part of the typical flower is the *stamen*. Often a flower has many stamens, each consisting of a slender stalk called a *filament* tipped with a round to oblong body called an *anther*. The anther contains many tiny grains of *pollen*, which usually look like yellow powder. Each microscopic grain contains one sperm cell that carries half the plant's genes.

The female part of the flower is the *pistil*. Often a flower has just one pistil, but it may have many, and they may be fused. Each pistil has three main parts: the *stigma* at the tip, designed to catch pollen grains; the stalk or *style* in the middle; and the *ovary* at the base. The ovary contains one to many *ovules*, each with an egg cell that carries half the plant's genes. An ovule becomes a *seed* when its egg cell is fertilized by a sperm cell. At the same time, the ovary (and sometimes other parts) surrounding the seed or seeds matures into a *fruit*. Fruits come in many forms, including fleshy berries, hard nutlets and pea-like pods.

The nonsexual parts of a flower help ensure successful *pollination*, which is the transfer of pollen from an anther to a stigma. A typical flower has two rings of structures surrounding its male and female parts. The outermost structure, the *calyx*, is made up of separate or fused *sepals*, which are usually green and leaf-like.

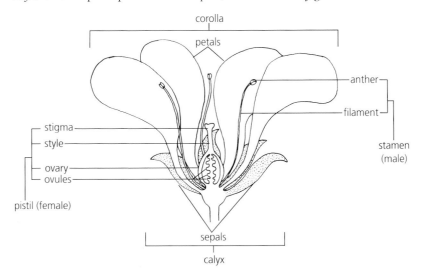

Sepals cover developing flower buds; they may also shelter mature flower parts and eventually protect the seeds. Within the calyx is the *corolla*, made up of separate or fused *petals*. Most of the colourful structures that we see in wild-flowers are petals, but sepals may also be showy.

Petals help protect the stamens and pistils, but their main function is to attract pollinators. A pollinator is an animal, usually an insect, that picks up pollen and carries it to a stigma. Petals aid pollination by catching the eye of potential pollinators, by providing landing platforms for flying visitors and by discouraging visits from insects that can't pollinate the flower. Many flowers also attract pollinators by giving off a strong smell and by producing pools of a sugary liquid called nectar. You'll be amazed at the great variety of colours and forms among common wildflowers, and at the intricate ways that pollinators and flowers depend on one another.

Floral Tricksters

Parts of a Flowerhead of the Aster Family

flowerhead

tubular floret

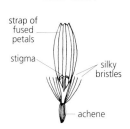

strap-like floret

If a plant has very tiny flowers, one way to attract a pollinator's attention is to produce large, eye-catching clusters. In some cases, these clusters have become so highly developed that they look just like single, large flowers, when they are really compact bouquets of tiny blooms. Flower clusters like these can be confusing when you first try to understand wildflower structure.

In this book, many of the wildflowers that use this trick to get attention belong to the aster family. These plants produce showy *flowerheads* made up of several to hundreds of tiny, stalkless flowers called *florets*. In some cases the petals of each floret are fused into a ribbon-like strap, but florets with tubes of fused petals are equally common.

Flowerheads can be made up entirely of strap-like florets (e.g., common dandelion, p. 71) or of tubular florets (e.g., Canada thistle, p. 65). Typically, however, a flower-head in the aster family has a central yellow 'button' of tubular florets surrounded by a showy ring of strap-like florets (e.g., oxeye daisy, p. 79). In such two-parted flowerheads, the strap-like florets are commonly mistaken for petals and the central tubular florets are mistaken for stamens. A cross-section of an aster flowerhead is shown at left, along with typical tubular and strap-like florets. A magnifying glass will help you see these structures in a real flowerhead.

Asters aren't the only tricksters among our common wildflowers. Bunchberry (p. 62), water calla (p. 61) and paintbrush (p. 39) have crowded their flowers into clusters or spikes and surrounded them with showy bracts that are often mistaken for petals.

Some floral tricksters. *Top left to right:* common dandelion (strap-like florets), Canada thistle (tubular florets), oxeye daisy (strap-like and tubular florets). *Below:* bunchberry and paintbrush (showy bracts).

Tips for Identifying Wildflowers

1. ***Stop and take a closer look.*** Each wildflower has its own distinctive character, but it's easy to miss important features if you can't see the details. Examine the flower or flower cluster. How big is it? How many petals does it have? Looking closely at a plant will help you with tips 2, 3, 4 and 5.

2. ***Decide which flower group your plant belongs to (pp. 18–19).*** Then, page through the corresponding section of the book until you find a plant like yours. You may need to understand the flower's structure to do this, so be sure to look closely and watch out for tricksters (see p. 12 and above).

3. ***Check the colour guide to the flowers (pp. 4–9).*** This handy section shows small photos of all 112 wildflowers in the guide arranged by colour for quick comparison. Flower colour can vary, so be sure to check the written description for possible variations if the picture doesn't seem quite right.

4. ***Try the illustrated wildflower key (pp. 26–35).*** Using a key is easy, once you get used to it. It is often a more precise way to identify a plant than a photo. If the key doesn't lead you to your plant, it will at least narrow your choices.

5. ***Check other books.*** This guide includes 112 common wildflowers, but hundreds of others also grow in Alberta. Many of these other species are close relatives of plants in this guide and look very similar. Even if this guide doesn't have the exact flower that you are trying to identify, it should give you an idea of the plant group (genus or family) to which it belongs. A list of reference books may be found on p. 153.

6. ***Don't hesitate to ask.*** Local naturalists and gardeners are usually happy to help you identify wildflowers, and they can often tell you stories about these fascinating plants.

To Pick or Not to Pick?

Wildflower lovers are often faced with an important question: To pick or not to pick? It is wonderful to take home a bouquet of fresh flowers and it's fun to press flowers for crafts or collections, but it would be wrong to strip our meadows and waysides of their beautiful blooms, leaving none for others to enjoy.

Most wildflowers that grow in open fields and on barren ground are hardy plants, capable of surviving and even thriving under extremely difficult conditions. Some, however, are surprisingly sensitive. For example, when you pick a wood lily, you take the leaves, stalk and all, and the plant dies. Introduced wildflowers tend to be weedier and less sensitive to cutting than native species. Often, introduced plants have adapted to a wide range of habitats and have very few natural enemies in their new home. The diseases and insects that preyed on them in Europe or Asia have usually been left behind. As a result, introduced weeds often spread rapidly, severely damaging crops and natural vegetation. These flowers can, and often should, be picked.

scentless chamomile

Some common wildflowers are considered to be harmful to people or property and have been classified as noxious or nuisance weeds. These plants are regulated by the Alberta Weed Act, the Canada Weed Control Act and the Canada Seeds Act. The legislation requires many such weeds to be destroyed if they grow close to land that is used for agriculture or horticulture or if they somehow interfere with such uses. The table on the next page lists the wildflowers in this guide that are classified as noxious or nuisance weeds.

Weedy species—especially those introduced from Eurasia—can usually be collected with little concern about quantities, and noxious weeds can be gathered freely if they are not poisonous or otherwise dangerous. On the other hand, many native wildflowers grow in sensitive habitats or can easily be killed by picking. These species should not be picked at all. Still other plants should be gathered only in moderation; for example, take just one flower in every 20.

This guide helps you decide whether or not you should pick a wildflower by providing a picking category for each plant (see p. 23).

If you pick an introduced wildflower, and especially one listed in the table on this page, avoid spreading its seeds. It's also best not to plant weedy introduced species in your garden, in case they spread to natural areas.

Always treat native plants with respect, and take only as much as you need. If you just want to press the flowers, take only the flowers and leave the rest of the plant to grow.

Noxious and Nuisance Weeds in This Guide

COMMON NAME	SCIENTIFIC NAME	PAGE NUMBER
spreading dogbane	*Apocynum androsaemifolium*	142
spotted knapweed	*Centaurea biebersteinii*	66
field mouse-ear-chickweed	*Cerastium arvense*	122
spotted water-hemlock	*Cicuta maculata*	98
Canada thistle	*Cirsium arvense*	65
field bindweed	*Convolvulus arvensis*	147
annual hawk's-beard	*Crepis tectorum*	68
tower larkspur	*Delphinium glaucum*	44
common viper's-bugloss	*Echium vulgare*	144
wormseed wallflower	*Erysimum cheiranthoides*	105
leafy spurge	*Euphorbia esula*	94
brittle-stem hemp-nettle	*Galeopsis tetrahit*	43
oxeye daisy	*Leucanthemum vulgare*	79
butter-and-eggs	*Linaria vulgaris*	38
meadow buttercup	*Ranunculus acris*	117
dock	*Rumex* spp.	104
bladder campion	*Silene vulgaris*	123
wild mustard	*Sinapis arvensis*	107
perennial sow-thistle	*Sonchus arvensis*	70
common tansy	*Tanacetum vulgare*	88
common dandelion	*Taraxacum officinale*	71
golden-bean	*Thermopsis rhombifolia*	52
scentless chamomile	*Tripleurospermum perforata*	80
white death-camas	*Zigadenus elegans*	112

Top left to right:
spreading dogbane,
tower larkspur,
leafy spurge.
Below:
common tansy and
field bindweed.

Danger, Beware!

A beautiful patch of wildflowers may demand a closer look, but before you rush over to investigate, take time to look around for possible dangers. Ditches often harbour broken glass and sharp sticks. Sudden drops may lie hidden under dense plant growth. Cacti and other spiny plants are easily overlooked until discovered by unprotected toes. When soil is bare, slopes can be unstable (especially when they're wet) and may start to slide from under you.

If you are looking at flowers near a road, remember to watch for passing vehicles. It's also unwise to use roadside plants for food or medicine. Plants growing along roads are usually exposed to many different pollutants. Vehicle exhaust and dust settle on plants; runoff from the road carries salt, oil and other pollutants to nearby soil; and pest-control programs can coat plants with herbicides and insecticides. All in all, it's safer and more enjoyable to study plants well away from heavy traffic.

Even in pristine areas, proceed with caution if you are using any plant for food or medicine. Poisonous plants can be confused with edible species. The carrot family (pp. 95–98) is especially dangerous. Some of our most poisonous plants (e.g., spotted water-hemlock, p. 98 and shown in photo, opposite) are very similar to edible plants (e.g., common water-parsnip, p. 97). Carelessly consuming plants in the carrot family is a sort of herbal Russian roulette. Never eat any part of a plant unless you are 100% sure of its identity.

Even with good identification, there can be problems. One person may be allergic to a berry that someone else eats all the time. People with special health considerations such as pregnancy or heart problems may be harmed by a plant that others can use safely.

Potentially harmful wildflowers are identified as such in this book. However, two other plants that harm people do not have showy flowers; their inconspicuousness, in fact, makes them more dangerous. Both can make your skin burn and itch. Learn to recognize these plants:

stinging nettle

Stinging nettle *(Urtica dioica)*. With its unassuming clusters of tiny, green to purplish flowers, stinging nettle blends in easily with other plants. It can usually be found in low meadows, ditches, gullies and other places where soils are rich and moist. The four-sided stems reach 1–3 m in height, much taller than most of the mint species with which this plant could be confused. Stinging nettle can be recognized by its opposite, slender-stalked leaves, which have coarsely toothed, lance-shaped to heart-shaped blades 4–15 cm long, and of course by its tiny stinging hairs if you are unfortunate enough to touch this plant. Each hollow hair has a swollen base that contains formic acid, the same chemical that gives attacking ants their sting.

When the hair pierces you, it injects the acid into your skin, causing itching or burning that lasts anywhere from a few minutes to a couple of days. Usually the effect lasts for less than an hour, but it can be very irritating. Don't panic. It should soon go away. Some say that rubbing the sting with the roots of the offending plant will help to reduce the burning, but this cure may be more psychological than physical.

Western poison-ivy *(Toxicodendron rydbergii).* Western poison-ivy is a low, bushy herb 10–40 cm in height, with a woody base. It prefers sunny, well-drained sites in ravines, on river flats and in open woods. The plants often form colonies by sending out creeping underground stems. In autumn, the leaves may turn bright red, and white, berry-like fruits may be seen. Poison-ivy is usually recognized by its long-stalked, three-parted leaves. The three pointed leaflets are 3–15 cm long and have smooth or slightly toothed edges. If you're not sure whether a plant is poison-ivy, just remember the rhyme 'Leaves of three, let it be.'

Western poison-ivy will deposit an irritating resin on anything it contacts. The resin can be removed by washing with strong soap and water, but if it is left on skin for more than about 5–10 minutes, it usually causes a rash. Pets, tools, clothing and even smoke from burning poison-ivy plants can carry the allergen to unsuspecting victims. Once the rash appears, ointments and antihistamines can help reduce the itching and swelling. Traditional treatments included applying dried blood or the sap from touch-me-not or stinging nettle. Sensitivity varies from one person to the next, and bad cases may require a visit to the doctor.

spotted water-hemlock

western poison-ivy

Organization of the Guide

This guide includes 112 wildflowers common along Alberta waysides, in pastures and in waste areas such as abandoned lots. Almost all are conspicuous even to highway travellers. A few less noticeable species (e.g., Virginia strawberry) are also included because they are so common.

Two features usually help us recognize flowers: colour and structure. All the wildflowers in this book are organized by colour in the colour guide to the flowers on pp. 4–9, but remember that flower colour can vary. For example, Canada violet (p. 45) may be pink at one site and white at another. Check the flower descriptions for the full range of colours.

Within the book, the wildflowers are divided into five major sections based on the structure of flowers or flower clusters:

Section 1: Two-Sided Flowers (pp. 36–57)
This section includes some of our most unusual flowers. These two-sided, or *bilaterally symmetrical*, flowers can be divided into two equal halves along only a single line. A good example of a two-sided flower is a violet.

lines of symmetry

violet, pp. 45, 46   bird's-foot-trefoil, p. 53   lady's-slipper, p. 36

Section 2: Tiny Stalkless Flowers in Compact Heads (pp. 58–90)
Some plants have tiny (1–5 mm wide), apparently stalkless flowers in dense, head-like clusters. These clusters, which often appear as individual flowers, are called *flowerheads*. A daisy, for example, is a flowerhead, not a single flower. (See 'Floral Tricksters,' p. 12.)

Most wildflowers in Section 2 belong to the large and variable aster family. These plants have flowerheads ranging from single, huge sunflowers to the scores of small flowerheads in goldenrods. The structure of a typical aster flowerhead is illustrated on p. 12.

There is some overlap between sections 1 and 2, because some members of the pea family (such as clovers, pp. 58–59) have tiny, two-sided flowers that form dense spikes and heads. These flowers are at the beginning of Section 2.

florets   flower-head   bracts

sunflower, p. 74   dandelion, p. 71   smartweed, p. 60   bunchberry, p. 62

Section 3: Tiny Stalked Flowers in Branched Clusters (pp. 91–105)

Many flowers are so tiny, you may need a magnifying glass to see them clearly. Even the tiniest blooms, however, become conspicuous if there are enough of them. The individual flowers in this section are only 1–5 mm wide, but dozens or even hundreds of them combine to form showy, lacy clusters.

| water-parsnip p. 97 | false-toadflax p. 99 | bedstraw p. 103 | dock p. 104 |

Section 4: Circular Flowers with Distinct Petals (pp. 106–141)

When most people think of a flower, they think of a plant from this section. Circular, or *radially symmetrical*, flowers can be divided into two equal parts along two or more lines. The circular flowers in Section 4 are more than 5 mm across and have corollas that are divided at least halfway to their bases, so their petals stand out clearly as individual parts. Section 4 includes a great variety of flowers, ranging from buttercups to lilies.

lines of symmetry

| flax p. 137 | blue-eyed-grass p. 110 | fireweed p. 139 | pond-lily p. 115 |

Section 5: Circular Flowers with Fused Petals (pp. 142–147)

This relatively small section includes funnel-shaped and bell-shaped flowers. These circular (radially symmetrical) flowers are more than 5 mm across and have corollas that are fused for more than half their length, creating a tube-like structure often tipped with the petal lobes.

lines of symmetry

| harebell p. 146 | bindweed p. 147 | dogbane p. 142 |

Information for Each Species

The following information is provided for each wildflower in this guide.

COMMON AND SCIENTIFIC NAMES

Each entry begins with a common name for the wildflower. This name is widely used and generally accepted in our region for that particular plant.

Most plants, and especially most widespread plants like the ones in this guide, have lots of common names. Many wildflowers have long histories, so it's not unusual for a species to have 20 or more common names. Different names can evolve in different regions, at different times and in reference to different uses or stories. You may already know some of these plants by other names.

The common name is followed by the scientific (Latin) name for the species. Although scientific names may be hard to pronounce and remember at first, they are much less confusing than common names in the long run. Generally, a species has only one accepted scientific name, and this name can be changed only when research shows that the original classification was wrong or that an earlier name was overlooked. Scientific names are much less changeable than common names because they have to be presented in reputable publications and accepted by taxonomists (scientists who study classification) before they can be established. Publication also helps keep track of all scientific names that have ever been used for a plant, so it's possible to trace the origins of these names and avoid confusion. Best of all, scientific names apply all over the world, so people who speak different languages can all use the same name.

The family name is also given for each species, in the coloured header bar at the top of the page. As the word suggests, a family is a group of related plants. Knowing which family a wildflower belongs to can help you recognize its relatives. For example, once you learn the general features of peas, you can go straight to the pea family (pp. 47–59) when you see a plant with those features. Common family names also have Latin counterparts: the table on p. 154 lists the common and scientific family names along with page ranges for quick reference.

blue giant-hyssop

NOTES

Below the names, each species entry presents some notes of interest about the wildflower. This section will vary greatly, but it includes the following types of information.

Natural History

Wildflowers depend on many different parts of their environment to survive and reproduce. Information about natural history could include interactions between plants and animals. For example, which animals use these plants for food or shelter? How do plants protect themselves from being eaten?

Many common flowers are successful colonizers, so some notes describe how they reproduce. Why has this wildflower succeeded where others have failed? How are its flowers pollinated to produce seed? How are its seeds carried to new sites? Can it spread in other ways? Many wildflowers have been spread around the world by human activities such as gardening, farming and shipping. Information about immigration tells when the plant arrived, where it spread and how, and whether it has become a troublesome weed.

annual sunflower

Human Uses

People have used wildflowers for centuries. A wide range of uses may be presented for a species, but it should be stressed that the reliability of the information varies greatly. Much of it comes from very old sources, and few of the uses have been studied by modern-day researchers.

Food and medicine. Many wildflowers have been important to people as food and medicine. The notes may describe where, when and how plants were collected, what parts were used and how they were processed. For example, were the plants eaten raw, pickled, steamed, boiled or fried? Were their healing properties extracted in teas, syrups or tinctures (alcohol extracts), or were plants simply applied in poultices or inhaled as smoke? Perhaps some plants required special preparation, such as removal of tough or spiny outer layers or soaking in lye to neutralize bitter chemicals.

Leaves, stems and buds may be added to salads, sandwiches, stews, soups, stir-fries, cakes, puddings, omelettes, cheeses and teas. Some have been used to thicken gravy or flavour liqueurs. Roots are occasionally eaten raw in salads, but usually they have been cooked as a vegetable or dried and ground into meal. Some roots have been used to make wine, tea or coffee and to flavour other dishes. Edible flowers and flower pollen are usually used simply as a garnish, but starchy, oil-rich seeds have been used widely for food. Many types of seeds can be gathered and ground into meal or flour for making gruel, cakes and breads. Still others can be roasted to make coffee-like drinks.

The wildflowers in this guide have been used to treat a wide array of ailments, from cuts, bruises and burns to dysentery, cancer and multiple sclerosis. Some have been used cosmetically to remove warts and pimples, and many have been used to treat everyday problems such as upset stomachs, headaches, cramps and colds. Over the years, many wild plants have been applied in poultices and lotions to relieve the aches of arthritis and rheumatism. Still others have been used in medicines for heart disease and diabetes. Remember that very few of these wide-ranging medicinal uses have been tested scientifically.

Wild plants should be used as food or medicine only with *extreme caution.* See the 'Danger, Beware' section on pp. 16–17 and the individual species entries for more information.

roadside wildflowers

Household uses. The range of uses for common plants seems to have been limited only by the imagination of industrious homemakers. Some of the wildflowers in this guide have been used for making soap, deodorant and insect repellent. Others have provided dyes, toys, cosmetics and stuffing for mattresses and pillows. Many have been used as a source of fibre for thread, cord, twine, cloth, rope and even fishnets. The notes may describe where, when and how plants were collected, what parts were used and how they were processed.

Farming. Some plants were brought to North America as sources of animal feed or green manure. The notes for these plants may include livestock preferences, nectar production (for honey) and the importance of plants in soil improvement programs.

Landscaping. Many successful wayside wildflowers are cultivated as hardy ornamentals. Still others are planted on exposed ground to stabilize slopes and enrich soil. The notes about these plants may include advantages or disadvantages of introducing a particular wildflower into your garden, and the importance of some species for landscaping parks and roadsides.

Superstitions and Folklore

Many myths, legends and superstitions have become associated with wild plants. Plant lore is especially well known for Eurasian species because stories have been written down for hundreds of years in that part of the world. Some wildflowers have been used as charms against snakes, witches and other perceived threats. Still other plants were chewed and rubbed onto bodies to provide strength, energy and protection from evil forces.

Meaning of Names

Most scientific names are based on Greek or Latin words. These strange-sounding words often tell us something about the history or appearance of the plant. By understanding the name, you can learn something about the wildflower and you may find the name easier to remember. If a name has changed recently, its previous name may be included at the end of the notes.

IDENTIFICATION POINTS

The bottom part of each species entry gives a short description of the plant, focusing on features that are important for identifying it: the colour, shape and size of the plant and its leaves, flowers and fruits. Most of the information in this section is presented in everyday language, but sometimes more technical terms have to be used. If you don't understand a word, look in the illustrated glossary (pp. 148–152) for an easy-to-understand explanation.

Size ranges are given for most of the identifying features. A ruler is printed on the back cover for quick reference.

Blooming times are also given, to let you know when you can expect to see each flower.

HABITAT AND DISTRIBUTION

For each wildflower, you will also find information about where to look for it. This information comes in two parts. The first, 'Habitat,' describes the type of ecosystem where the wildflower usually grows. Most of the plants in this guide thrive on disturbed ground such as roadsides, but many also grow in more natural habitats such as meadows, woods, streambanks and lakeshores. 'Habitat' is followed by 'Distribution,' which describes the geographical range. If the wildflower grows here naturally, this section begins with the word 'native.' If the species has been intro-

yellow marsh-marigold

duced from elsewhere in the world, its distribution begins with the region where it originated, followed by the parts of North America (north of Mexico) in which it now grows wild.

PICKING GUIDELINE

At the very end of the species description, you will find a general guide to how many blooms it is acceptable to pick:

Pick none: for sensitive native wildflowers or those that grow in sensitive habitats. Don't pick these at all, and avoid trampling them.

Pick a few: for common native plants. Take a few blooms, but be sure to leave many more behind for others to enjoy.

Pick freely: for abundant, weedy plants (mainly introduced), some of which are noxious or nuisance weeds. Take all you want!

Some of the plants in this guide may be dangerous to pick because they are poisonous or have spines, hairs, sap or pollen that can irritate skin. These species have the word **caution** in the 'Pick' part of the description. For example, the picking guideline for Canada thistle is 'freely; caution' because this plant is a noxious weed but is covered in sharp spines—take all you want, but look out for the prickles. Yellow marsh-marigold, on the other hand, is sensitive to picking and its sap can irritate sensitive skin. Its picking code is 'none; caution'—you shouldn't pick it, but you wouldn't want to, anyway.

Of course, these categories apply to plants that are well established in the wild. In some regions, wildflowers are planted along highways to add beauty to barren landscapes and to stabilize and improve soils. If an area has been seeded recently, its young plants should be left alone to multiply.

Fun with Flowers

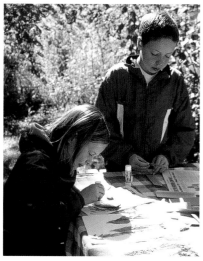

Wildflowers add beauty to fields and waysides, and they add interest to trips and outings. When kids are travelling, it's fun to keep track of all of the different wildflowers along the way. See who can find the first orange, red or purple wildflower, or who can spot the most species in 10 kilometres, in 10 minutes or all day.

As you get to know wildflowers, you may want to keep track of which ones you've seen. All of the species in this guide are listed alphabetically by common name in a checklist on p. 155.

It's hard to identify flowers when you're zooming along at highway speed, and it's dangerous to stop on busy roads. Take time for short walks at roadside pullouts and parks: you'll be surprised at what you discover. Better yet, follow the road less travelled. Back roads let you enjoy a relaxed pace and pull over more easily.

Closer to home, get to know the wildflowers in your neighbourhood and watch them as they grow. You may enjoy keeping a nature diary with notes, sketches and pressed leaves and flowers, describing how plants change through the summer and from year to year. Plants are very cooperative: they stay in the same place throughout their lifetime, and they stand still while you examine them, making them excellent subjects for drawings, paintings and photos.

Everyone enjoys bouquets of freshly cut flowers, and some wildflowers will last for days if they're treated properly. Flowers need to be put into water as soon as possible so they don't wilt. When you pick a plant, it continues to try to draw water up its stem, and air is sucked into the little tubes that carry liquid to the flower. Just before you put your bouquet into water, cut off the bottom few centimetres of each stem to trim off the airlock and allow water to move up the stem to nourish the flowers and leaves. Try adding food colouring to the water, and watch white blooms magically change colour.

With luck, fresh flowers can last for a week, but dried flowers remain beautiful for months or even years. Some flowers preserve better than others. For example, blanketflower and tansy flowers dry well, but more delicate blooms such as golden corydalis and wild blue flax soon fade. Fruit clusters such as the shiny brown capsules of bladder campion and the 'fairy candelabras' of old crane's-bill pods also add interest to winter bouquets and wreaths.

Many common wildflowers can be dried by simply hanging them in bundles in a warm, dark, dry place. Generally, the more quickly a flower dries, the better its colour will be. If the bundles become too hot, their flowers can scorch and fade, but if they are too cool or damp they may turn brown or mould.

Another way to dry wildflowers is to press them between sheets of absorbent paper such as newsprint. Simply lay the flower between two sheets of paper on a flat surface, put another flat surface over the paper and set a weight on top. Often people press plants in books, but this doesn't always work well; very little air gets to the plant, so the flowers and leaves may mould, and the book can be damaged. For better results, make your own plant press. Simply use pieces of corrugated cardboard for your flat surfaces and then alternate layers of cardboard, paper, plants, paper, cardboard and so on. When you've laid all your flowers in place, strap or tie the layers together in a snug bundle and set it in a warm place to dry. Air will pass through the tunnels in the cardboard, drying the flowers quickly so that they keep their colour. If the flowers are bulky, you may need to put a weight on top to help flatten them. If you can't get everything to lie the way you want it to, try pressing the flower for a few hours, and then carefully rearrange the petals and leaves while they are still damp.

Pressed flowers are easy to store, and they can be used in many ways. A wildflower collection is a wonderful memento of a trip. Each flower can remind you of a special stop along the way. It's a good idea to write the name of each plant and the place and date you collected it on the pressing paper.

Many craft projects can make use of pressed flowers. The flowers can be glued to paper and covered with clear plastic to make beautiful notecards and bookmarks. Pressed flowers can also be arranged on cardstock and framed behind glass. Similarly, dried wildflowers set between two sheets of glass make lovely wall hangings, sun-catchers and decorations. Pressed clusters of water-parsnip flowers look just like delicate snowflakes, perfect for winter holiday decorations.

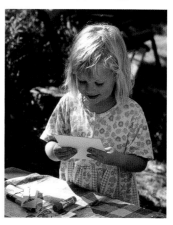

The possibilities are endless—just use your imagination!

Using a Key to Identify Wildflowers

A quick and easy way to identify wildflowers is to use a key. Keys ask you questions about the flower you are trying to identify, and you provide the answers. Each answer leads you either to another question or to the name of the wildflower. By using a key, you can narrow your possibilities without having to look through the entire book.

This is a *dichotomous* key, which simply means that the choices are in pairs so you always choose between two alternatives. For example, read 1a and 1b. If the flowers are tiny (1–5 mm across), 1a is right, so you go to choice 2: 2a or 2b. If the flowers are larger, 1b is correct, so you go to choice 11: 11a or 11b. Eventually, you should come to an illustration of your flower. Turn to the page number indicated for that flower to learn more about it.

You can sometimes reach the same answer in more than one way. For example, you may look at a daisy and think that it is a single flower, but someone else may know that it is really a flowerhead made up of many tiny flowers. Some of these potential problems have been taken into consideration in this key, so that you can identify the daisy either way.

If you don't understand some of the words used in the keys or elsewhere in the guide, check the illustrated glossary (p. 148).

Key to the Wildflowers in This Book

Note: In this key, 'petals' refers to all petal-like structures, including true petals, petal-like sepals, petal-like bracts and petal-like florets.

1a Flowers or flower-like heads tiny, usually 1–5 mm across . . . go to 2a/2b

1b Flowers or flower-like heads larger (over 5 mm across), single or in showy clusters . . . . go to 11a/11b

2a Flowers in head-like clusters or spikes; individual flowers stalkless or stalks too short to be seen . . . . go to 3a/3b

2b Flowers in looser clusters that are branched and often lacy; individual flowers or small (1–5 mm) flowerheads clearly stalked . . . go to 10a/10b

3a Flower clusters appearing to be individual flowers, made up of a dense central clump of tiny flowers surrounded by a ring of showier, petal-like flowers or bracts . . . . go to 4a/4b

3b Flower clusters head-like, made up of tiny flowers that are all similar . . . . go to 6a/6b

4a   Flowerheads large and showy, usually at least 2 cm across
. . . . go to **5a/5b**

4b   Flowerheads smaller, 0.5–2 cm across, but forming showy branched clusters

sweet-colt's-foot
p. 87

ragwort
p. 86

spike-like goldenrod
p. 92

Canada goldenrod
p. 93

yarrow
p. 91

spurge
p. 94

5a   'Petals' yellow or orange

sunflower
p. 74

blanketflower
p. 75

gumweed
p. 78

false-golden-aster
p. 77

coneflower
p. 76

5b   'Petals' white, pink or blue

bunchberry
p. 62

oxeye daisy, p. 79
chamomile, p. 80

American-aster, pp. 82, 83
wood-aster, p. 81

fleabane
pp. 84, 85

6a   Each tiny flower not flat and petal-like, usually pea-like or with a tube of fused petals, but sometimes too tiny to tell . . . . go to **7a/7b**

6b   Each tiny flower appearing to be a single flat petal, its true petals fused into a ribbon-like strap

wild lettuce
p. 67

hawkweed, p. 69
hawk's-beard, p. 68

sow-thistle, p. 70
dandelion, p. 71
false-dandelion, p. 72

goat's-beard
p. 73

7a 'Petals' expanded and showy .... go to **8a/8b**

7b Petals inconspicuous, often hidden by bristles or absent altogether

burdock
p. 64

pineappleweed
p. 89

tansy
p. 88

pussytoes
p. 90

calla
p. 61

strawberry-blite
p. 63

8a Each tiny flower funnel-shaped and/or 2-lipped (not tubular), often with enlarged, spreading 'petals' .... go to **9a/9b**

8b Each tiny flower with a slender, hair-like tube of fused petals

burdock
p. 64

thistle
p. 65

knapweed
p. 66

9a Flowers in whorls at stem tips or in leaf axils

beardtongue
p. 100

mint
p. 102

giant-hyssop
p. 101

9b Flower clusters otherwise, at stem or branch tips

sweet-clover
p. 56

alfalfa
p. 57

clover
pp. 58, 59

smartweed
p. 60

10a Flower clusters somewhat elongated, usually tapered to a point at the tip

| Canada goldenrod p. 93 | wallflower p. 105 | false-toadflax p. 99 |

| bedstraw p. 103 | spike-like goldenrod p. 92 | dock p. 104 |

10b Flower clusters wide, with flat or rounded tops, often umbrella-shaped

| water-parsnip p. 97 | water-hemlock, p. 98 cow-parsnip, p. 96 | heart-leaved Alexanders, p. 95 |

| yarrow p. 91 | spurge p. 94 |

11a Flowers or flower-like clusters 2-sided (bilaterally symmetrical), divisible into 2 equal parts along a single line through the centre, usually with an upper and a lower lip . . . . go to **12a/12b**

11b Flowers or flower-like clusters round or star-shaped (radially symmetrical), divisible into 2 equal parts along 2 or more lines through the centre . . . . go to **16a/16b**

12a Flowers or flower clusters with sac-like, spurred and/or fused petals or 1 large bract . . . . go to **13a/13b**

12b Flowers violet- or pea-like, with 5 separate petals including 1–2 upper petals, 2 side (wing) petals and a lower lip formed by 1–2 petals . . . . go to **14a/14b**

13a Flowers somewhat funnel-shaped, with all petals fused for at least half their length into a cone or tube

giant-hyssop p. 101	hemp-nettle p. 43	hedge-nettle p. 42
butter-and-eggs p. 38	wild bergamot p. 41	paintbrush p. 39

13b Flowers otherwise, not funnel-shaped; petals or petal-like bracts fused only at base, if at all

calla p. 61	lady's-slipper p. 36	corydalis p. 37	bladderwort p. 40	larkspur p. 44

14a Petals pink, blue or purple .... go to **15a/15b**

14b Petals yellow or white

violet p. 45	golden-bean p. 52	bird's-foot-trefoil p. 53	locoweed p. 55
sweet-clover p. 56	alfalfa p. 57	clover pp. 58, 59	licorice p. 54

15a Flowers in elongated clusters

vetchling p. 50	milk-vetch p. 51	sweet-vetch p. 47	vetch pp. 48, 49

15b Flowers single or in compact, head-like clusters

violet pp. 45, 46	alfalfa p. 57	clover pp. 58, 59

16a 'Petals' separate for at least half their length, appearing as distinct petals or scales . . . . go to **17a/17b**

16b Petals fused for more than half their length to form tubes, funnels or bells

dogbane p. 142	viper's-bugloss p. 144	gromwell p. 143

bluebells p. 145	harebell p. 146	bindweed p. 147

17a Flowers or flowerheads with more than 10 'petals' . . . . go to **18a/18b**

17b Flowers or flowerheads with 10 or fewer 'petals' . . . . . . go to **22a/22b**

18a Flowerheads with a ring of broad 'petals' around a distinctly different centre of anthers or tubular florets . . . . go to **19a/19b**

18b Flowerheads composed of 1 type of 'petal' or tiny flower . . . . go to **20a/20b**

19a 'Petals' yellow or orange

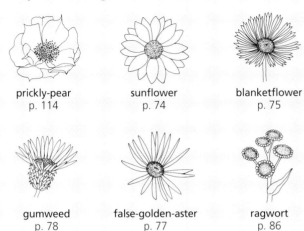

prickly-pear
p. 114

sunflower
p. 74

blanketflower
p. 75

gumweed
p. 78

false-golden-aster
p. 77

ragwort
p. 86

19b 'Petals' white, pink or blue

oxeye daisy, p. 79
chamomile, p. 80

American-aster, pp. 82, 83
wood-aster, p. 81

fleabane
pp. 84, 85

sweet-colt's-foot
p. 87

20a 'Petals' hair-like to egg-shaped but not strap-like . . . . . go to **21a/21b**

20b 'Petals' flattened, strap-like

wild lettuce
p. 67

hawkweed, p. 69
hawk's-beard, p. 68

sow-thistle, p. 70
dandelion, p. 71
false-dandelion, p. 72

goat's-beard
p. 73

21a 'Petals' slender and tubular, often almost hair-like

knapweed
p. 66

thistle
p. 65

burdock
p. 64

pussytoes
p. 90

21b 'Petals' broader, often tapered to a point, not hair-like

alfalfa
p. 57

clover
pp. 58, 59

paintbrush
p. 39

22a Flowers or flowerheads with 3–10 showy 'petals' . . . . . go to **23a/23b**

22b Flowers or flowerheads with 0–2 showy 'petals'

strawberry-blite
p. 63

burdock
p. 64

pineappleweed
p. 89

tansy
p. 88

spurge
p. 94

23a Flowers or flowerheads with 4, 5 or a varying number of up to 10 'petals'; flower parts not arranged in threes . . . . go to **24a/24b**

23b Flowers with 3 or 6 'petals'

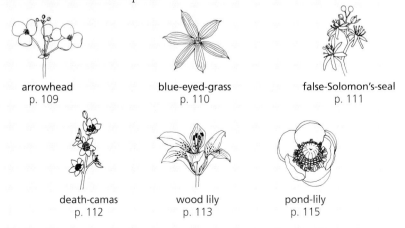

arrowhead
p. 109

blue-eyed-grass
p. 110

false-Solomon's-seal
p. 111

death-camas
p. 112

wood lily
p. 113

pond-lily
p. 115

24a Flowers or flowerheads with 5–10 'petals' (coneflower variable, occasionally with 3–4) . . . . go to **25a/25b**

24b Flowers or flowerheads cross-shaped, always with 4 'petals'

wild mustard
p. 107

tumbleweed mustard
p. 106

bunchberry
p. 62

fireweed
p. 139

evening-primrose
p. 140

25a Flowers and leaves alternately attached (1 per stem joint) or basal
. . . . go to **26a/26b**

25b Flowers and leaves paired (2 per stem joint)

campion
p. 123

mouse-ear-chickweed
p. 122

yellow-loosestrife
p. 124

26a 'Petals' not yellow . . . . go to **27a/27b**

26b 'Petals' yellow

mountain-avens
p. 129

marsh-marigold
p. 116

buttercup
pp. 117, 118

yellow avens
p. 127

silverweed, p. 130
plains cinquefoil, p. 132

shrubby cinquefoil, p. 131
graceful cinquefoil, p. 133

mullein
p. 141

coneflower
p. 76

27a 'Petals' white

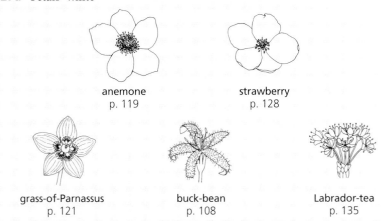

anemone
p. 119

strawberry
p. 128

grass-of-Parnassus
p. 121

buck-bean
p. 108

Labrador-tea
p. 135

27b 'Petals' orange, red, pink, blue or purple

globe-mallow
p. 138

crane's-bill
p. 136

rose
p. 134

flax
p. 137

prairie-crocus
p. 120

three-flowered
avens, p. 126

shootingstar
p. 125

prairie-crocus

Yellow Lady's-Slipper

Cypripedium parviflorum

This beautiful orchid is widespread but never common, so it is always an exciting discovery. You may be tempted to transplant lady's-slippers to your garden, but please leave them for others to enjoy. Orchid roots grow with special fungi (mycorrhizae) that help them take nutrients from the soil. If the orchid's specific fungus doesn't grow in your garden, neither can the orchid. • The unusual flowers are designed to trap insects. Bees and flies enter easily through the mouth of the slipper, but once inside they slide down smooth, steep walls. Eventually, they discover a hairy strip and follow it

out, but along the way they must first hit the stigma (female part) and then pick up a sticky clump of pollen from the male part. • This species has also been called *C. calceolus*.

Plant: erect perennial 20–80 cm tall, from fibrous roots Leaves: oval to lance-shaped, 6–20 cm long, with sheathing bases Flowers: with 4 (3 separate, 2 fused) purplish brown to greenish yellow, 3–8 cm tepals around a yellow, 2–5 cm, pouched lip; 1–2 flowers per stalk Blooms: May to July Fruits: oblong capsules containing some 15,000 seeds Habitat: moist roadsides and woodlands Distribution: native across North America and around the world Pick: none

Golden Corydalis

Corydalis aurea

This low-growing, early-blooming wildflower flourishes on newly broken ground, but it soon disappears as other plants move in. • Golden corydalis was sometimes used as medicine. Some tribes inhaled the smoke from smouldering roots to clear congestion. Others used the sprawling, grey-green plants to make teas for illnesses ranging from sore throats, stomachaches and headaches to bronchitis, dysentery and heart disease. Many of the alkaloids in golden corydalis are similar to those in the opium poppy, so they have been intensively studied. Unfortunately, some of these compounds are also poisonous. No one has yet died from eating golden corydalis, but large quantities can cause trembling, staggering and convulsions. • Gardeners have soaked watermelon seeds in golden corydalis tea to increase production. • This plant is sometimes called scrambled-eggs.

Plant: much-branched annual or biennial, with sprawling to ascending stems 20–50 cm long, from slender taproot **Leaves:** mostly twice pinnately divided into 3-lobed leaflets 1–3 cm long **Flowers:** golden yellow, 1–1.6 cm long, tubular, with a 4–5 mm pouch (spur) at the base; flowers in compact clusters 1–3 cm long **Blooms:** May to July **Fruits:** slender, cylindrical pods 1.5–2.5 cm long, narrowed between shiny black, 2 mm seeds **Habitat:** open, often rocky sites **Distribution:** native from Quebec to Alaska to West Virginia and Texas **Pick:** a few

Butter-and-Eggs
Linaria vulgaris

Butter-and-eggs is a native of Asia and became popular in Europe as a hardy ornamental plant that added a lot of colour and needed little care. It has been very successful on our continent, where it spreads rapidly by seed (up to 8700 per plant) and by creeping underground stems. • Its acrid juice makes butter-and-eggs distasteful to animals and potentially poisonous to humans. In Scandinavia, the plants were boiled in milk to make an insecticide used for attracting and poisoning flies. • Only large insects, such as honeybees and hawk moths, are strong enough to open the lips of these flowers and have tongues long enough to reach the nectar. If you hold a flower up to the light, you can see the nectar in its spur. • This plant is sometimes called toadflax, a name that in Old English translated as 'useless flax.'

Plant: erect, greyish green perennial 30–80 cm tall, from creeping roots **Leaves:** many, alternate (lower leaves sometimes paired), slender, tapered to a stalk-like base, 2–6 cm long **Flowers:** snapdragon-like, 2–3.5 cm long, yellow with an orange lower lip and a slender, yellow, backward-pointing tube (spur); many flowers in compact spikes **Blooms:** May to September **Fruits:** rounded, 8–12 mm capsules containing winged seeds **Habitat:** dry, disturbed ground **Distribution:** Eurasia; naturalized from Newfoundland to Alaska to Texas **Pick:** freely

Common Red Paintbrush

Castilleja miniata

The vivid colour of red paint-brush comes, not from petals, but from brightly coloured bracts that hide most of the true flowers. • Sweet nectar makes these tender flowers a tasty trail nibble, and the 'paintbrushes' have been added to salads and sandwiches. However, these plants can accumulate toxic amounts of selenium, so they are probably best left alone. • Some tribes mashed paintbrush plants with grease and used the mixture to make their hair healthy and glossy. The effectiveness of this hair dressing could have been related to its selenium content. • Paintbrushes have green leaves and produce their own food, but they also join roots with neighbouring plants to steal water and nutrients. Common red paintbrush would look lovely in the garden, but it has to grow with a suitable host plant. Transplanting almost never succeeds.

Plant: erect perennial 20–60 cm tall, with somewhat woody base Leaves: 3-nerved, slender to lance-shaped, 2–7 cm long, sometimes shallowly 3-lobed at the tip, stalkless Flowers: green with red edges, tubular, 2–3.5 cm long, with a slender, arching upper lip and a tiny, 3-lobed lower lip; flowers largely hidden by broad, showy, rose to scarlet or yellowish bracts tipped with 1–5 lobes, forming dense spikes Blooms: June to September Fruits: capsules 9–12 mm long Habitat: open, well-drained sites Distribution: native from Ontario to Alaska to Arizona Pick: a few

Greater Bladderwort

Utricularia macrorhiza

You may be pleasantly surprised to discover clusters of small, yellow, snapdragon-like flowers on ponds and in ditches. These flowers may seem unusual, but the most exciting part of the plant lies hidden underwater. Bladderworts are carnivorous plants, and their leaves form some of the most sophisticated traps in the plant kingdom. In the greater bladderwort, some leaflets form elastic-walled bladders no more than 5 mm across. When a tiny aquatic animal, such as a protozoan, swims by, trigger hairs cause a flap-like door to spring open, sucking the unsuspecting passerby into the bladder. The flap closes and then the plant quickly digests its prey. Within an hour or two, the animal is gone and the trap is reset. • The bladders gave rise to the genus name, from the Latin *utriculus*, 'small bottle.' *U. macrorhiza* has also been called *U. vulgaris* var. *americana*.

Plant: floating aquatic perennial with branched stems 30–80 cm long
Leaves: underwater, 2–5 cm long, repeatedly pinnately divided into slender segments, many with bladders 3–5 mm long
Flowers: yellow with brown stripes on the upper lip, snapdragon-like, 1.5–2.5 cm long; in clusters of 6–15, held well above the water on stout stems **Blooms:** June to August **Fruits:** small capsules on arching stalks **Habitat:** calm water
Distribution: native from Newfoundland to Alaska, south through the U.S. **Pick:** none

Wild Bergamot

Monarda fistulosa

European settlers and Native peoples gathered this aromatic plant for flavouring salads, cooked vegetables and stews and for making a pleasant minty tea. Dried, powdered leaves were sprinkled on food to keep flies and other insects away and were rubbed onto hair, skin, clothing and even favourite horses as perfume. The plant's fragrance was likened to that of bergamot (the citrus used to flavour Earl Grey tea), giving rise to the name wild bergamot. Settlers soon began planting this beautiful, useful herb and introduced it to England in 1744 as an edible ornamental and a flavouring for tea. Since then, many hybrids have been developed, providing a variety of long-lasting, rose pink to deep red blooms for bouquets of cut flowers. • Wild bergamot will attract butterflies and hummingbirds to the garden. It is best grown from seed.

Plant: grey-green, square-stemmed perennial 50–120 cm tall, from spreading rootstock **Leaves:** paired, lance-shaped, toothed, stalked, 6–10 cm long, smaller upwards **Flowers:** lavender to purple or yellowish pink, 2–3.5 cm long, tubular, with a 3-lobed lower lip and a slender, fuzzy, 2-lobed upper lip tipped with 2 projecting stamens; flowers in head-like clusters **Blooms:** June to September **Fruits:** 4 small nutlets **Habitat:** upland wooded and open sites **Distribution:** native from Quebec to B.C. to the southern U.S. **Pick:** a few

Hairy Hedge-Nettle

Stachys pilosa

Hairy hedge-nettle is a showy, hardy perennial that makes an attractive addition to wildflower gardens, but beware! The spreading rootstock can quickly carry the plant to places it isn't wanted. • Although this hedge-nettle is rather fuzzy, unpleasant-smelling and bitter-flavoured, all parts of the plant are reputed to be edible. Young plants are the most tender, and boiling helps to reduce the smell, so usually young shoots were cooked. The plump, crisp rootstocks were collected in autumn and eaten raw, boiled, baked or pickled. • Hairy hedge-nettle was once used in poultices, ointments and syrups to stop bleeding, heal wounds and relieve cramps, joint pain and dizziness. However, its main qualification as a healing herb was its disagreeable, 'medicinal' smell. • *S. pilosa* is sometimes included in *S. palustris*, which is called marsh hedge-nettle.

Plant: soft-hairy, often glandular perennial 30–100 cm tall, with 4-sided stems
Leaves: paired, 3.5–9 cm long, blunt-toothed, mostly stalkless **Flowers:** pale rose to purplish or whitish, with red blotches, 1.1–1.6 cm long, funnel-shaped, with a hooded upper lip and a flared, 3-lobed lower lip; borne in circles (whorls) of 2–6 in loose spikes 5–15 cm long
Blooms: June to August **Fruits:** 4 nutlets
Habitat: wet sites **Distribution:** native from Quebec to Alaska to the southern U.S. and around the world **Pick:** a few

Brittle-Stem Hemp-Nettle

Galeopsis tetrahit

This prickly immigrant was common in Canada by 1884. Today, it is classified as a weed in Alberta, Manitoba, Quebec and Alaska. • In European kitchens, the stems, roots and flowers were used to make a tea and to season meat. The leaves provided a spring potherb. In merry old England, distilled water from hemp-nettle flowers was said to make the heart glad, the face rosy and the vital spirits fresh and lively. Similarly, plants boiled in wine were applied as hot plasters to remove hardness from the spleen (the seat of melancholy). Modern-day herbalists usually suggest brittle-stem hemp-nettle as a remedy for coughs and congestion, a tonic for blood disorders, a sedative for hyperactive children, an appetite stimulant and a breath freshener. For relief from severe hiccups, try chewing a few hemp-nettle leaves.

Plant: bristly-hairy annual 30–80 cm tall; stems coarse, with swollen joints
Leaves: paired, ovate to lance-shaped, 3–12 cm long, coarse-toothed, stalked
Flowers: pink, white or variegated, often with 2 yellow spots, tubular, 1.5–2.2 cm long, with a rounded upper lip and 3-lobed lower lip; flowers whorled in upper leaf axils, often forming spikes **Blooms:** July to August **Fruits:** 4 nutlets in an enlarged 5–11 mm long calyx with 5 spine-tipped lobes **Habitat:** open, disturbed sites
Distribution: Eurasia; naturalized from Newfoundland to B.C. to the northern U.S.
Pick: freely

Tower Larkspur
Delphinium glaucum

In some parts of North America, this beautiful wildflower is one of the most common causes of livestock poisoning. Cattle are especially susceptible, but horses rarely eat enough to cause symptoms, and sheep seem immune. In fact, sheep are sometimes used to control tower larkspur. • Larkspurs contain alkaloids that can cause stomach upset, nervous problems, depression and even death. Young plants are most poisonous. Toxicity decreases with age, reaching one-half by flowering time and one-sixteenth when the fruits mature. The seeds, however, are extremely poisonous. • At one time, ground larkspur seeds and flowers were steeped in alcohol or vinegar, and the resulting extract was used to kill body lice. Larkspur soap killed head lice. These remedies were dangerous if applied to broken skin.

Plant: hairless, blue-green perennial 50–200 cm tall, from stout rootstock
Leaves: 10–20 cm across, deeply cut into 5–7 wedge-shaped, lobed segments arranged like fingers on a hand (palmate)
Flowers: dark blue to purplish, about 2–2.5 cm long, with 5 spreading, petal-like sepals and 4 small, pale, inconspicuous petals; upper sepal tapered to a slender, backward-pointing spur; flowers in spike-like clusters **Blooms:** July to August
Fruits: erect groups of 2–3 hairless pods (follicles) 1–1.4 cm long **Habitat:** moist, open sites **Distribution:** native from Saskatchewan to Alaska to Arizona
Pick: a few; caution

Canada Violet

Viola canadensis

Some tribes tell of a mythical hero who fell in love and stole a girl from her tribe. As the couple fled, the girl wound her braids around her neck to show that she and her lover were married, and her enraged tribe killed them both on the spot. The following spring a new flower, the violet, appeared with the girl's hair etched on its petals. The violet became a symbol of love, courage and devotion, known as 'heads entangled.' • Fine lines on violet petals guide insects to nectar in the spur via a path that ensures pollination. If no pollinators arrive, the violet produces tiny, scentless flowers later in the summer. These never open but rather pollinate themselves, thus ensuring a seed crop. • Each seed has an oily part that ants find irresistible. The ants carry seeds to their nests, eat the oily bits and discard the rest, thereby planting new violets. • *V. canadensis* has also been called *V. rugulosa*.

Plant: perennial 10–40 cm tall, from ascending to creeping rootstock **Leaves:** heart-shaped, 2–10 cm long, coarsely toothed, mostly long-stalked **Flowers:** white to pale pink, with purplish veins and a yellow throat, 1.5–2.5 cm across, 2-lipped, with 5 separate petals and a 4–6 mm backward-pointing spur; side-petals hairy; flowers single in upper leaf axils **Blooms:** April to July **Fruits:** egg-shaped capsules **Habitat:** moist woods and meadows **Distribution:** native from Newfoundland to Alaska to Georgia and Arizona **Pick:** a few

Early Blue Violet

Viola adunca

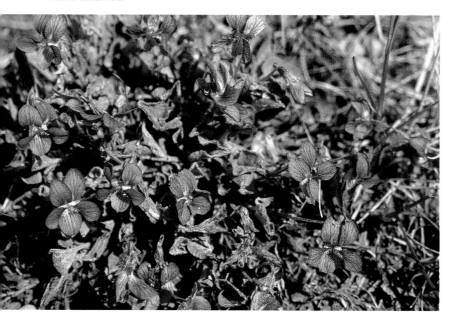

Early blue violet's delicate blossoms hold one of the loveliest wildflower fragrances. Enjoy it while you can. The flower's perfume doesn't fade, but your sense of smell is soon dulled by a substance called ionine. In a few moments the perfume returns, only to disappear again just as quickly.
• The leaves and flowers of all violets are edible, but many wild species are too small for gathering. Violet flowers make beautiful garnishes in salads or punch bowls. They can also be candied or used to make purplish jelly and vinegar. • Violet leaves contain more vitamin A than spinach, and one-half cup of violet leaves offers as much vitamin C as four oranges.

Plant: low perennial 2–8 cm tall when flowering
Leaves: basal and on flowering stalks, heart-shaped, usually 1–2.5 cm wide, blunt-toothed; stalks with 2 slender, toothed lobes (stipules)
Flowers: purple to blue with a white throat, 2-lipped, with 5 separate petals and a 4–6 mm backward-pointing spur, side-petals hairy, 8–15 mm long; flowers single on slender stalks **Blooms:** May to July **Fruits:** 4–5 mm long capsules, shooting out brown seeds **Habitat:** moist to dry, sandy or gravelly sites **Distribution:** native from Labrador to Alaska, south through the western U.S. **Pick:** a few

American Sweet-Vetch

Hedysarum alpinum

The 'sweet' in sweet-vetch could refer to the beautiful, fragrant flowers of these plants or to the sweet, edible roots. American sweet-vetch roots are best from autumn to spring, when they contain stored sugars and other nutrients for the plant. As the growing season progresses, these food reserves support the rapidly growing plant, and the roots become tough and dry. When the plant shuts down for winter, it moves nutrients back to the roots for winter storage, and they soon grow crisp and sweet again. • These nutritious, carrot-flavoured roots were a popular food and trade item among Native peoples and were eaten raw, boiled, baked or fried. American sweet-vetch roots are also a favourite food of bears, lemmings and mice. Mice sometimes store large quantities, and people learned that an easy way to gather roots in winter was to train their dogs to sniff out mouse caches hidden under the snow. • This plant has also been called alpine sweet-vetch and *H. americanum*.

Plant: perennial, with erect or ascending stems 15–80 cm long, from taproot **Leaves:** with prominent veins on the lower side, pinnately divided into 11–21 leaflets; leaflets 1–3 cm long **Flowers:** reddish purple to pinkish, pea-like, 1–1.8 cm long; hanging in elongated clusters **Blooms:** June to August **Fruits:** flattened, winged pods, narrowed and jointed between seeds, usually 4–6-seeded **Habitat:** open, well-drained sites **Distribution:** native from Newfoundland to Alaska to the northern U.S.; also in Asia **Pick:** a few

American Vetch

Vicia americana

The name *Vicia* comes from the Latin *vincio*, 'to bind together,' referring to the twining tendrils of these plants. • Sometimes American vetch is confused with veiny vetchling *(Lathyrus venosus)* because both are twining legumes with reddish purple, pea-like flowers. The easiest way to tell a vetch from a vetchling is to look at the tiny style between the two lower petals. In vetches, the style tip has a bottle-brush cluster of hairs, whereas in vetchlings the hairs are all on one side, so the style looks like a tiny toothbrush. • Tender young American vetch plants were sometimes baked or boiled as greens, but this common wildflower was not widely used. Some tribes steeped the roots to make a love medicine; others blew smoke from burning plants into the nostrils of horses to increase the animals' endurance.

Plant: climbing perennial 20–80 cm tall, often in tangled masses **Leaves:** pinnately divided into 8–14 leaflets plus 2 toothed, semitriangular stipules at the base and a well-developed, forked tendril at the tip; leaflets strongly veined, 1.5–3.5 cm long, pointed **Flowers:** reddish purple (drying blue), pea-like, 1.5–2.5 cm long, with a pointed keel much shorter than the side-petals; 2–9 flowers in loose, elongating clusters **Blooms:** June to July **Fruits:** flat, hairless pods 2–4 cm long, with dark, round seeds **Habitat:** open to semishaded sites, often in woods **Distribution:** native from Quebec to Alaska to Texas **Pick:** a few

Bird Vetch
Vicia cracca

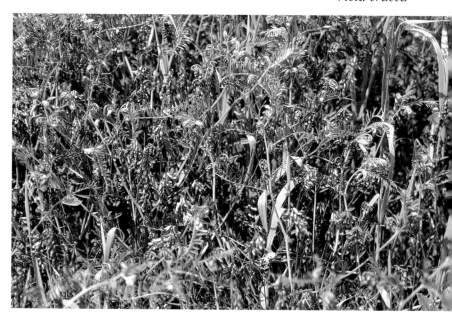

This abundant weed often goes unnoticed until it bursts into bloom in midsummer. Bees and butterflies flock to the nectar-rich flowers. When an insect lands, its weight forces the flower's inner parts to flip out from the lower lip. The female part then brushes pollen from the insect's belly, and the male part applies a fresh dusting of pollen. Pollinated flowers soon close, darken and point downwards. The mature pods burst when touched, each side recoiling tightly. You may not see the seeds shoot out, but you often hear them landing. • The young plants, pods and seeds are occasionally eaten, but they must be boiled first to destroy their toxins.

Plant: twining, grey-green perennial up to 1 m tall **Leaves:** pinnately divided, with 1–3 tendrils at the tip and 10–24 smooth-edged, sharp-pointed leaflets below, plus 2 lobes (stipules) at base of stalk **Flowers:** blue to lavender (rarely white), narrowly pea-like, 8–13 mm long, with unequal sepals and a bottle-brush-tipped style; flowers in dense, 1-sided clusters **Blooms:** June to August **Fruits:** slender, pea-like pods 2–2.5 cm long, each containing 5–8 seeds **Habitat:** disturbed ground **Distribution:** Eurasia; naturalized across North America **Pick:** freely

Cream-Coloured Vetchling

Lathyrus ochroleucus

Many members of the pea family are poisonous, but there is little information about the toxicity of most wild species. Early settlers considered cream-coloured vetchling a 'locoweed,' and therefore bad for horses, but some Native peoples fed it to their ponies to make them lively for races. Although this vetchling can provide some fodder, it is less palatable than many other plants and its seeds may be poisonous. Some tribes used the roots for food and medicine, but given the questionable toxicity of vetchlings in general, such uses are not recommended. • The roots have nodules containing bacteria that convert nitrogen from the air into a form that plants can use, so cream-coloured vetchling helps to enrich soil.

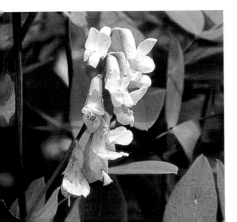

Plant: sprawling perennial, with slender stems up to 1 m long **Leaves:** tipped with tendrils and pinnately divided into 6–10 oval leaflets 2–5 cm long, plus 2 large, almost heart-shaped lobes (stipules) at the stalk base **Flowers:** yellowish white, pea-like, 1.2–1.8 cm long; hanging in 5–10-flowered clusters from leaf axils **Blooms:** May to July **Fruits:** pea-like pods about 4 cm long **Habitat:** moist, open or wooded sites **Distribution:** native from Quebec to Alaska, south to the northern U.S. **Pick:** a few

American Milk-Vetch

Astragalus americanus

The rather pleasant name milk-vetch refers to the historical belief that these plants increased milk production in goats and cows. However, many milk-vetches are poisonous and are more appropriately called locoweeds (like their *Oxytropis* cousins; see p. 55). Unfortunately, records of poisonous and nonpoisonous species are incomplete for this large genus of about 1500 species. • Some milk-vetches cause locoism, a type of insanity, in livestock (see p. 55). Many species also accumulate selenium and molybdenum, which are toxic in large quantities. In fact, prospectors often use milk-vetches as indicators of selenium and associated minerals. • Some tribes used American milk-vetch roots as famine food and as a remedy for nausea, cramps and worms, but given its unknown toxicity, this plant is best left alone. • *A. americanus* has also been called *A. frigidus* var. *americanus*.

Plant: erect perennial 50–100 cm tall, from branched, woody base **Leaves:** pinnately divided into 7–15 elliptic leaflets 2–4 cm long **Flowers:** yellowish white, pea-like, 1.3–1.5 cm long; flowers numerous, in clusters 5–10 cm long **Blooms:** July to August **Fruits:** hanging, thin-walled, inflated pods 1.5–2 cm long, on 5–10 mm stalks **Habitat:** moist, often shady sites **Distribution:** native from Quebec to Alaska to Colorado; rare from Manitoba eastward **Pick:** a few

Golden-Bean
Thermopsis rhombifolia

Each spring, golden-bean's sunny yellow blossoms bring long-awaited splashes of colour to road-sides and meadows across the Prairies. Native peoples especially welcomed the early arrival of this lovely wildflower. Its appearance marked the beginning of the season when bison bulls were in their prime—hence another common name, buffalo-bean. During this period, the bulls began leaving their winter range for summer grazing on the plains, and hunters moved to intercept them. • Though there are a few reports of medicinal uses for golden-bean, this plant is poisonous and should never be eaten or used in internal medicines. The seed pods look like little peas, a resemblance that may tempt children to eat them, but golden-bean can cause severe illness and even death if enough beans are swallowed.

Plant: erect perennial 10–50 cm tall, with branched stems; often forming large patches from creeping rootstocks
Leaves: divided into 3 leaflets plus 2 large leaflet-like lobes (stipules) at the stalk base; leaflets narrowly egg-shaped, 2–4 cm long
Flowers: bright golden yellow, pea-like, 1–2 cm long; in short clusters **Blooms:** May to June **Fruits:** flattened pods 3–7 cm long, often curved in a semicircle; containing 10–13 seeds **Habitat:** well-drained, open sites **Distribution:** native from Ontario to B.C. to New Mexico **Pick:** a few

Bird's-Foot-Trefoil

Lotus corniculatus

This cheerful roadside wild-flower was brought to North America for fodder and honey. In the Middle Ages, bird's-foot-trefoil was recommended as a potherb, but eventually it fell out of favour, perhaps because the raw leaves and flowers contain cyanide. Nineteenth-century herbalists began recommending the plant as a sedative when a distressed woman tried to use it to treat her inflamed eyes and instead found herself somehow cured of insomnia and heart palpitations. No medicinal uses have been clinically proven. • *Corniculatus*, meaning 'small horn,' may refer to the tiny, pointed seed pods. Many fanciful common names for this weed compare its slender, spreading pods to toes or fingers. 'Trefoil' comes from the Latin *tria foliola*, which means 'three leaflets'—though the leaves of this particular trefoil are divided into five leaflets.

Plant: erect to sprawling perennial 10–60 cm tall **Leaves:** with 5 ovate, 5–15 mm long leaflets (3 at the tip and 2 near the stalk base) **Flowers:** bright yellow, sometimes tinged red, pea-like, 1–2 cm long; 3–6 flowers in flat-topped clusters on slender, 5–10 cm stalks **Blooms:** June to August **Fruits:** slender pods about 2.5 cm long, palmately arranged **Habitat:** moist, disturbed sites **Distribution:** Eurasia; naturalized across temperate Canada and through the U.S. **Pick:** freely

American Licorice

Glycyrrhiza lepidota

For centuries, the thick, sweet-tasting roots of American licorice have provided food and medicine. The flavour and active ingredients in American licorice are similar to those of Eurasian licorices *(G. glabra, G. uralensis)*, and these plants have been used in many of the same ways. People chewed licorice root as a sweet, thirst-quenching nibble, or they used it to flavour candies, root beer and tobacco. Roasting concentrates the flavour. • For thousands of years, *Glycyrrhiza* species have been among the most popular medicines in China. Licorice has often been used to flavour bad-tasting preparations, and studies have confirmed its effectiveness in treating asthma, bronchitis and stomach ulcers. It was even shown to be as effective as codeine for controlling coughs. However, licorice should always be used in moderation. Large doses can raise blood pressure.

Plant: coarse, erect perennial 30–100 cm tall, from taproot and creeping rootstock **Leaves:** dotted with glands, pinnately divided into 11–19 leaflets; leaflets lance-shaped, 2–4 cm long, abruptly sharp-pointed **Flowers:** yellowish white, pea-like, 1–1.5 cm long; in dense, erect, 2–6 cm long clusters from leaf axils **Blooms:** May to July **Fruits:** reddish brown, bur-like pods 1–2 cm long, covered in dense, hooked bristles **Habitat:** open, moist, well-drained sites **Distribution:** native from Maine to B.C., south through the U.S. **Pick:** a few

Showy Locoweed

Oxytropis splendens

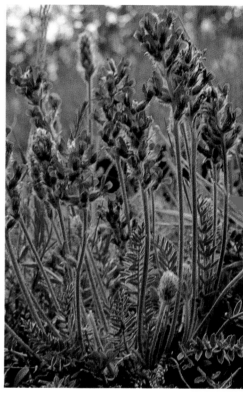

Locoweeds are readily distinguished from other flowers in the pea family by the sharp point at the tip of the keel—the lower pair of petals hidden between the two wing petals. In fact, the genus name *Oxytropis* comes from the Greek *oxys*, 'sharp,' and *tropis*, 'keel.' • The Blackfoot called locoweed 'rattleweed' because they used the seeds in ceremonial rattles, and because ripe seed pods rattle when shaken. Rattleweed tea was given to children with asthma, especially if their breathing rattled. • *O. splendens* is one of our prettiest locoweeds. It is easily identified by its purplish flowers and its silver-haired, whorled leaflets. This showy plant thrives in dry, exposed sites, so it makes an excellent addition to dry prairie gardens. • The name locoweed refers to the reputed ability of these plants to drive animals crazy. Livestock will often become addicted to locoweed and eat fatal quantities.

Plant: tufted, silky-hairy perennial 7–35 cm tall, from deep taproot **Leaves:** basal, 7–26 cm long, with oblong-elliptic to lance-shaped leaflets in 7–15 pairs or groups, at least a few in whorls of 3–6 **Flowers:** reddish purple to blue, pea-like, 1–1.5 cm long; 12–35 flowers in dense clusters 3–10 cm long **Blooms:** July **Fruits:** woolly, egg-shaped pods 8–17 mm long **Habitat:** open, well-drained sites **Distribution:** native from Ontario to Alaska to New Mexico **Pick:** a few

Sweet-Clover

Melilotus officinalis

Sweet-clover is a hardy, drought-resistant forage crop, known for its ability to improve poor soils. It is also highly valued as a honey plant, hence the name *Melilotus*, from the Greek *meli*, 'honey.' Its abundant, fragrant blossoms produce large amounts of nectar. Once pollinated, a plant can produce as many as 350,000 seeds, some even capable of surviving for more than 80 years. • Sweet-clover leaves and flowers emit a vanilla-like scent and have been used to enhance desserts and drinks, especially teas. The leaves also flavour Gruyère cheese, snuff and tobacco. Only dried plants should be used for these purposes. Mouldy sweet-clover contains the toxic anticlotting agent dicoumarin, which was used to develop the rodent poison warfarin. • White-flowered sweet-clover has been called *M. alba*.

Plant: slender, taprooted biennial (sometimes annual) 50–200 cm tall, with branched stems **Leaves:** with 3 oblong to lance-shaped, blunt-tipped, 1–2.5 cm leaflets that are sharply toothed on the upper half **Flowers:** yellow or white, narrowly pea-like, 4.5–7 mm long; in many narrow clusters 3–8 cm long **Blooms:** May to September **Fruits:** egg-shaped pods about 3 mm long, usually 2-seeded **Habitat:** open, disturbed ground **Distribution:** Europe; naturalized across North America **Pick:** freely

Alfalfa
Medicago sativa

Alfalfa is a valuable fodder and green-manure plant that originally came from western Asia. It was planted in Greece as early as 490 BC; Spanish conquistadors later introduced it to Mexico and Chile. Nowadays, alfalfa is perhaps best known for its tender, delicately flavoured sprouts, which are popular in salads and sandwiches. The mature plants are rich in protein, trace minerals, vitamins (A, C, D, E and K), folate and fibre. They have been used to make a nutritious but rather tasteless tea for treating many ailments, from water retention to cancer, though none of these medicinal uses has been clinically proven. • Alfalfa should be consumed in moderation because it contains substances that may affect liver function and sensitivity of the skin to sun. • 'Alfalfa' is a Spanish word originally derived from the Arabic *al-fasfasah*, 'best fodder.'

Plant: deep-rooted perennial up to 1 m tall
Leaves: with three 1.5–3 cm leaflets (each tipped with teeth) and 2 slender, toothed lobes (stipules) at base of stalk
Flowers: violet blue (var. *sativa*) or yellow (var. *falcata*), 6–12 mm long, on 2–3 mm stalks, narrowly pea-like, with 5 petals and 5 slender sepals; flowers in dense, round to cylindrical, stalked clusters **Blooms:** June to September **Fruits:** small pods, tightly coiled in 1.5–4 turns (var. *sativa*) or hooked or straight (var. *falcata*) **Habitat:** disturbed ground **Distribution:** Eurasia; naturalized across North America **Pick:** freely

Alsike Clover

Trifolium hybridum

Carpets of alsike clover stabilize the poor soils along many roads. This plant also improves the soil because clover roots have small nodules with specialized nitrogen-fixing bacteria (see p. 50). • Alsike clover is widely planted for fodder, food and medicine. The whole plant is rich in protein but difficult to digest, especially in large quantities; boiling helps. The tender white flower bases make a sweet nibble, and the dried flowerheads are used to make tea or are ground into flour. Research suggests that blood thinners found in clover may be useful for treating heart disease. • Each so-called 'flower' is actually a compact cluster of many tiny tubular flowers. These flowerheads bloom from the bottom up, and once pollinated, the flowers droop down, forming a skirt around the base of the cluster.

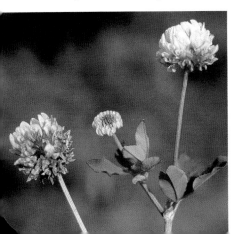

Plant: perennial 30–80 cm tall **Leaves:** with 3 blunt-tipped, elliptic leaflets and 2 conspicuous, slender-tipped lobes (stipules) at base of stalk; upper leaves with shorter stalks **Flowers:** pinkish to white (brown with age), 7–10 mm long, distinctly stalked, narrowly pea-like, with 5 petals and 5 slender sepals; flowers in head-like clusters on 2–8 cm stalks **Blooms:** May to August **Fruits:** inconspicuous, 1–6-seeded pods **Habitat:** disturbed ground **Distribution:** Eurasia; naturalized across North America **Pick:** freely

Red Clover

Trifolium pratense

If you're looking for a lucky four-leaved clover, try searching in a patch of red clover. Not only are four-parted leaves more common in this species, they are also extra large. This European native is often planted for forage and for green manure. Its long, tubular flowers depend on long-tongued bumblebees for pollination, so when red clover was introduced to New Zealand and Australia, crops failed until bumblebees were imported, too. This species is seldom used for food today, but whole plants, young leaves and flowers are all said to be edible, though difficult to digest. Never consume red clover in the fall, when the plants may look normal but contain toxic compounds.
• Red clover has long been used medicinally, as an ingredient in cough remedies and as a sedative, tonic and anticancer agent.

Plant: short-lived perennial up to 80 cm tall
Leaves: with 3 ovate leaflets (broadest above the middle) and 2 slender-pointed basal stalk lobes (stipules); upper leaves short-stalked **Flowers:** magenta to almost white, 1.3–2 cm long, stalkless, narrowly pea-like, with 5 petals and 5 slender sepals; flowers in stalkless or short-stalked heads 1.3–2.5 cm long **Blooms:** May to August
Fruits: inconspicuous, 1–6-seeded pods
Habitat: disturbed ground
Distribution: Europe; naturalized across North America **Pick:** freely

Water Smartweed

Polygonum amphibium

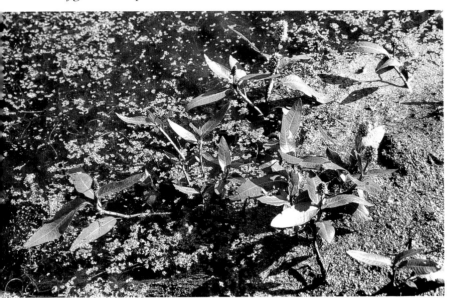

This widespread aquatic plant grows wild on every continent except Australia. It is an important food for migrating waterfowl, which carry its seeds around the world. • Some tribes used these beautiful pink flower clusters as trout bait, while others dried and smoked them as a hunting charm to attract deer. • The name *Polygonum*, from the Greek *polys*, 'many,' and *gonu*, 'knee,' refers to the knobby stems. Because of its 'many-kneed' appearance, Europeans once thought that smartweed was good for treating swollen, painful joints. Water smartweed is rich in astringent tannins and in flavonoids that slow bleeding and lower blood pressure. Native peoples used this plant to treat mouth sores, stomachaches, diarrhea and even peyote poisoning. • Water smartweed has also been called swamp persicaria.

Plant: aquatic to terrestrial perennial, with spreading 50–100 cm stems from rootstock **Leaves:** somewhat leathery, floating or spreading, 5–15 cm long; stalks with basal lobes forming a 1–2 cm long cylinder around the stem **Flowers:** bright pink to scarlet, with 5 petal-like sepals; flowers numerous, in 1–3 cm, oblong to egg-shaped spikes **Blooms:** July to August **Fruits:** dark brown, 2.5–3 mm, lens-shaped, seed-like achenes **Habitat:** calm, shallow water and shores **Distribution:** native from Newfoundland to Alaska, south through the U.S. and around the world **Pick:** none

Water Calla
Calla palustris

All parts of this beautiful plant contain tiny, sharp crystals of calcium oxalate. In the mouth and digestive tract, these crystals inflame soft tissues and cause an intense burning sensation. Because of this, animals rarely take more than one mouthful. • Despite the plant's fiery-hot nature, calla berries and rootstocks have been used for food. In Scandinavia, rootstocks were dried, ground, boiled and then mixed with powdered fir inner bark and baked in loaves. The resulting 'missen bread' was said to be as tough as rye bread but sweet and white. • Some tribes believed that people who wetted their hands with the milky root juice of water calla could safely handle rattlesnakes. • *Calla* comes from the Greek *kallos*, 'beautiful.' The ancient name water-dragon seems equally appropriate.

Plant: aquatic perennial, from creeping rootstock **Leaves:** basal, ovate to heart-shaped, 5–10 cm long; stalks 7–20 cm long
Flowers: tiny, yellowish, lacking petals and sepals; many flowers in a 1.5–2.5 cm long cylinder (spadix) at the base of a showy, white bract (spathe); spathe white, abruptly pointed, 2.5–7 cm long **Blooms:** June to July **Fruits:** red, berry-like, in dense heads 1.5–5 cm long **Habitat:** calm, shallow water
Distribution: native from Newfoundland to Alaska to the northeastern U.S. and around the world **Pick:** none; caution

Bunchberry

Cornus canadensis

Bunchberry makes a lovely groundcover in shady wildflower gardens. Each cheerful little 'flower' is, in fact, a miniature bouquet of tiny blooms surrounded by four showy bracts that look like petals. The bright white bracts lure pollinators to the true flowers, which are so tiny that they are easily overlooked. The bracts also provide landing platforms for insects carrying pollen from other plants. In late summer, dense clusters of small, red berries replace the flowers. Some people enjoy these juicy fruits, with their crunchy little seeds, but others consider them mealy and tasteless. Bunchberries can be eaten as a trail nibble or added to puddings and sauces.

Plant: colonial perennial 7–20 cm tall, from creeping rootstock **Leaves:** 4–8 cm long, with deep, arched veins; in circles (whorls) of 4–6 at stem tips **Flowers:** tiny, greenish yellow to purplish, clustered at centre of 4 white, petal-like bracts; each flower-like cluster 2–4 cm across **Blooms:** late May to July
Fruits: red, berry-like drupes, 6–8 mm long, in tight clusters **Habitat:** moist, often acidic sites **Distribution:** native from Newfoundland to Alaska to the northern U.S. and in eastern Asia and Greenland **Pick:** a few

Strawberry-Blite

Chenopodium capitatum

Strawberry-blite's eye-catching, bright red fruit clusters are juicy, sweetish and quite nutritious. They can be eaten raw as a trail nibble or salad garnish, or cooked as a colourful addition to soups, stews and other dishes. Young plants can be substituted for spinach in most recipes. Like spinach, which is also in the goosefoot family, they are very nutritious but should be eaten in moderation. • If you decide to dine on strawberry-blite, take care! Some believed that eating the flowers would make you as fat as if you were pregnant, and then all of your friends would laugh at you. More probably, the juicy fruits will stain your fingers and clothing a bright red. • Different tribes crushed strawberry-blite flower clusters with water to make pink ink for writing, red paint for adorning the face and body, and red dye for decorating baskets, rawhide, wood and quills.

Plant: succulent, yellowish green annual 10–50 cm tall **Leaves:** often reddish, broadly triangular, 2–12 cm long, with toothed or wavy edges **Flowers:** red, tiny, with 3–5 fleshy sepals; flowers in dense, round, 5–15 mm, pulpy clusters from leaf axils or in patchy spikes at stem tips **Blooms:** June to August **Fruits:** fleshy, with a single, black, lens-shaped seed 0.7–1.2 mm long **Habitat:** open, disturbed sites **Distribution:** native from Quebec to Alaska to Arizona and around the world **Pick:** a few

Woolly Burdock
Arctium tomentosum

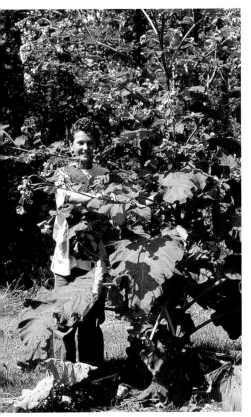

All burdocks have flower bracts tipped with hooked bristles that can catch on passing animals and carry seed heads to new sites. Some people claim that these bristles inspired the invention of Velcro. • The fleshy taproots of first-year plants can be eaten raw or boiled. They have a sweet, artichoke-like flavour when cooked. Burdock roots have also been dried, roasted and ground as a coffee substitute. The white stem pith is edible raw, cooked or even simmered in sugar to make candy. *Note:* Pregnant women and diabetics should not use burdock. • The broad leaves provided poultices for skin problems, and burdock seeds have been applied to bruises, venomous bites, abscesses and smallpox sores. • Woolly burdock can be easily distinguished from greater burdock *(A. lappa)* and lesser burdock *(A. minus)* by the abundant white, woolly hairs in its bristly flowerheads.

Plant: coarse biennial 80–300 cm tall, with tough, hollow stems from deep taproot
Leaves: white-woolly underneath, up to 50 cm across, heart-shaped, stalked
Flowerheads: bur-like, cobwebby-hairy, with slender, pink or purplish tubular florets at the tip of a round, 1.5–2.5 cm wide cluster of hooked bracts; flowerheads in branched clusters **Blooms:** July to October
Fruits: seed-like achenes 5–6 mm long
Habitat: disturbed sites
Distribution: northern Europe; naturalized mainly from Newfoundland to Alberta to Illinois **Pick:** freely

Canada Thistle

Cirsium arvense

Despite its name, Canada thistle is not a native plant. It arrived here from Eurasia in the 1700s and spread south to the U.S., where it was given its common name. • This is our only thistle with colonies of male or female plants. Deep underground runners shoot out rapidly—up to 6 m per plant per year—sending up as many as 200 shoots in the first summer. New shoots often stand in lines radiating from the parent plant, but soon they grow their own runners, and the area becomes blanketed in a thistle maze. One female plant can produce up to 40,000 seeds, each one capable of surviving 20 years or more. Not only can thistles reproduce rapidly, they have protective spiny leaves that are usually left to flourish, undisturbed by grazing animals.

Plant: prickly perennial 30–150 cm tall
Leaves: sometimes white-woolly underneath, wavy-edged or lobed, spiny-toothed
Flowerheads: rose purple to white, 1.5–2.5 cm across; florets all tubular, above a 1–2 cm cup of overlapping, pointed to spine-tipped bracts; flowerheads in branched clusters
Blooms: June to September **Fruits:** seed-like achenes with white, feathery bristles
Habitat: disturbed sites **Distribution:** Eurasia; naturalized from Newfoundland to Alaska to New Mexico **Pick:** freely; caution

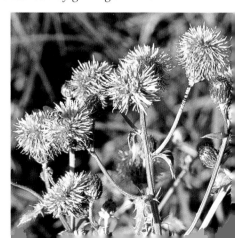

Spotted Knapweed

Centaurea biebersteinii

Spotted knapweed is a permanent member of many top 10 lists for noxious weeds. In Canada, it was first reported from Victoria, B.C., in 1893, and by 1932 it was found in Quebec. Although spotted knapweed is easily controlled by plowing, it has infested hundreds of thousands of acres of rangeland in North America. These plants spread only by seed, but one plant can produce more than 20,000 seeds, each a potential new colony. Plants begin growing early in spring, and this head start helps them outstrip other species in the race for moisture, nutrients and light. Once established, they give off chemicals to prevent other plants from growing nearby. • *C. biebersteinii* has also been called *C. maculosa*.

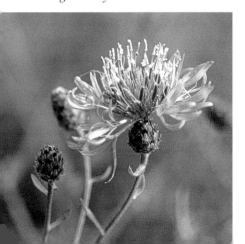

Plant: much-branched biennial or perennial 30–100 cm tall, sometimes with thin, cobwebby hairs **Leaves:** pinnately cut into slender lobes **Flowerheads:** pink-purple, 2–2.5 cm across; florets all tubular, but outer florets enlarged and spreading; flowerheads many, each with a 1–1.3 cm cluster of ribbed, black-fringed bracts **Blooms:** June to September **Fruits:** seed-like achenes **Habitat:** disturbed sites **Distribution:** Europe; naturalized in eastern and western Canada and across the U.S. **Pick:** freely

Common Blue Lettuce

Lactuca tatarica

The scientific name *Lactuca*, from the Latin word *lac*, 'milk,' refers to the milky sap of lettuce plants. This sap was said to heal pimples and other skin problems and to soothe stings. People who have sensitive skin, however, may develop rashes from lettuce sap.
• Although these plants have been eaten raw in salads or cooked as potherbs, their milky juice soon becomes very bitter, and older plants are quite tough. Some tribes dried sap from the roots, rolled it into balls and chewed it like gum.
• Common blue lettuce is sometimes grown from seed in wildflower gardens, but plant with caution. It often becomes weedy, and its deep, creeping rootstocks make it hard to control. • This species has also been named *L. pulchella*. *Lactuca* species are sometimes called horseweeds, because horses are said to favour them.

Plant: erect, blue-green perennial 20–80 cm tall, from rootstock **Leaves:** slender, 5–18 cm long, often with a few backward-pointing lobes, stalkless **Flowerheads:** blue, up to 2.5 cm across, with 18–50 strap-like florets above a 1–2 cm long tube of green bracts; flowerheads in open, branched clusters
Blooms: July to September **Fruits:** seed-like achenes 4–7 mm long, tipped with a stout beak bearing a parachute of silky white hairs
Habitat: moist, open, often disturbed sites
Distribution: native from Nova Scotia to Alaska, south through the U.S. and around the world **Pick:** a few; caution (irritating sap)

Annual Hawk's-Beard

Crepis tectorum

Annual hawk's-beard was introduced to the New World from Siberia. Back in 1877, it was first recorded in Canada in New Brunswick, and today the yellow flowerheads of this successful invader dot roadsides across North America. One plant can produce more than 49,000 seeds, each able to sprout almost as soon as it hits the ground. Annual hawk's-beard is considered to be a troublesome weed in Manitoba and Alberta, but it rarely becomes a problem in cultivated fields. Instead, it usually invades forage crops, pastures and roadsides. • Although the leaves of various hawk's-beards have been eaten (usually cooked), some European species are believed to cause nervous disorders, so these plants are better left alone. • Annual hawk's-beard has also been called narrow-leaved hawk's-beard.

Plant: erect annual 10–50 cm tall, with branched stems from taproot
Leaves: lance-shaped, 10–15 cm long, edged with backward-pointing teeth or pinnate lobes; smaller and simpler upwards
Flowerheads: yellow, 1–1.5 cm across, with 30–70 strap-like florets above a 6–9 mm high cluster of inwardly hairy bracts; 5 to many flowerheads in open, flat-topped clusters **Blooms:** June to July
Fruits: burgundy, seed-like achenes 3–4 mm long, spindle-shaped, 10-ribbed, tipped with a parachute of whitish hairs
Habitat: open, usually disturbed sites
Distribution: Eurasia; naturalized across North America **Pick:** freely

Narrow-Leaved Hawkweed

Hieracium umbellatum

This common wildflower could be confused with annual hawk's-beard (p. 68), but hawk's-beard has smaller (1–1.5 cm wide) flowerheads, paler green flower bracts and white (not tawny) hairs on its fruits. • The cut leaves and broken stems and roots of hawkweeds exude a milky sap (latex) that is rich in rubber. Some tribes chewed dried balls of sap or simply the plants themselves like chewing gum. • Although hawkweeds' flowerheads attract pollinating insects, they can often seed without fertilization. This type of reproduction (apomixis) can create classification nightmares for scientists by producing thousands of almost identical plants. More than 2400 minor species of *Hieracium* have been described from Britain and Scandinavia. • This species has also been called Canada hawkweed and *H. scabriusculum*.

Plant: erect to ascending perennial 20–100 cm tall, with milky sap and leafy stems **Leaves:** narrowly oblong to ovate, 3–8 cm long, toothed to almost smooth-edged; upper leaves often clasping the stem **Flowerheads:** bright yellow, 2–2.5 cm across; florets all strap-like, above an 8–12 mm high cluster of smoky green to blackish, overlapping bracts; flowerheads 1 to many in open clusters **Blooms:** July to September **Fruits:** ribbed, seed-like achenes 3 mm long, tipped with a tuft of soft, brownish hairs **Habitat:** open, often disturbed sites **Distribution:** native from Nova Scotia to B.C. to the central U.S. and around the world **Pick:** a few

Perennial Sow-Thistle

Sonchus arvensis

Some say the young shoots and leaves of perennial sow-thistle provide one of the best wild salads, but older leaves and flower buds are best boiled for 5–10 minutes. The bright yellow flowerheads provide a colourful garnish. • This common weed spreads rapidly. A single plant can produce 4000 seeds, which mature in only 10 days and can survive for several years. Once they establish, the fleshy, white roots spread horizontally, sending up new shoots. The roots are easily broken, and even small pieces can produce new plants. Additional roots stretch down as deep as 3 m. Sow-thistle competes enthusiastically for nutrients, moisture and light, so even minor infestations can drastically reduce crop yields. • Sow-thistle was so named because pigs apparently like to eat it.

Plant: erect, often blue-green perennial 40–200 cm tall, with milky sap
Leaves: 6–40 cm long, with prickly, deeply lobed edges; smaller, less lobed and clasping upwards on the stem
Flowerheads: yellow, 3–5 cm across; florets all strap-like, above overlapping rows of slender green bracts; flowerheads in widely branched clusters
Blooms: July to October **Fruits:** wrinkled, 10-ribbed, seed-like achenes tipped with silky white parachutes **Habitat:** disturbed sites **Distribution:** Europe; naturalized from Newfoundland to Alaska to Texas
Pick: freely

Common Dandelion

Taraxacum officinale

This successful immigrant has been planted for food and medicine since ancient times in Europe, China and India. The tender young leaves, rich in vitamins and minerals, make good salad or cooked greens. The delicate yellow flowers can be added to fritters and pancakes or made into wine. Dandelion roots provide a raw or cooked vegetable, a caffeine-free coffee substitute and even a red dye. With age, the plants soon grow bitter; leaves in full sun are especially harsh. Pale plants (like those grown in shade or buried in sand) and frost-nipped plants are sweetest. The mildly laxative and diuretic leaves have been used in medicinal teas, digestive aids, diet drinks and rustic beers.

Plant: robust perennial with milky juice, 5–50 cm tall, from taproot **Leaves:** basal, 5–40 cm long, irregularly toothed and lobed **Flowerheads:** yellow, 2–5 cm across; florets all strap-like, above 2 rows of slender, green bracts, the outer row bent backwards; flowerheads single on leafless, hollow stalks **Blooms:** April to September **Fruits:** spiny-ribbed, seed-like achenes with a slender, stalk-like beak bearing a silky white parachute **Habitat:** disturbed sites **Distribution:** Eurasia; a cosmopolitan weed **Pick:** freely

Pale False-Dandelion

Agoseris glauca

When false-dandelions are damaged, they exude lots of milky sap that is rich in rubbery compounds. Some tribes broke the plants, allowed the sap to coagulate and rolled it into balls. These balls were then chewed like gum, either for pleasure or as a tooth cleaner. People in a hurry simply chewed the whole leaf. These uses gave rise to another common name, Indian bubblegum. • The thick white sap, called latex, contains many waste products from the growing plant. Latex was once thought to help the plant heal wounds, but it is probably more important for protection from grazing animals. Pale false-dandelion provides forage for sheep and deer, but cattle and horses prefer other plants. Consequently, abundant false-dandelion growth usually indicates overgrazing and poor range conditions. • Pale false-dandelion has also been called pale goat-chicory.

Plant: blue-green perennial 10–45 cm tall, with erect, leafless stems from taproot
Leaves: basal, slender, 5–25 cm long, sometimes with scattered teeth or lobes
Flowerheads: light yellow (often drying pinkish), 2–5 cm across, single; florets all strap-like, above a cluster of slender, pointed, overlapping basal bracts
Blooms: June to July **Fruits:** seed-like achenes 5–12 mm long, tipped with a stout, ribbed beak bearing a cluster of silky white hairs **Habitat:** moist, open sites
Distribution: native from Ontario to Alaska, south to New Mexico **Pick:** a few

Common Goat's-Beard

Tragopogon dubius

Look for common goat's-beard early and late in the day. Its flowerheads usually open at sunrise and close by midday, but the large, fluffy seed heads are most visible in the evening, when their silky hairs catch the rays of the setting sun. The names goat's-beard and *Tragopogon* (from the Greek *tragos*, 'billy goat,' and *pôgôn*, 'beard') both refer to the fluffy tufts of hair on the seeds. These downy parachutes can carry seeds over great distances on the breeze, rapidly spreading goat's-beard to new areas. • Tender young goat's-beard shoots can be eaten raw or cooked, in the same way as asparagus, and the plant bases are sometimes cooked like artichokes. Also, the fleshy roots of first-year plants have been roasted or boiled like parsnips, or chopped raw and added to salads.

Plant: erect biennial 30–100 cm tall, with milky sap **Leaves:** grass-like, tapered from a clasping base to a slender point **Flowerheads:** yellow, 2.5–6.5 cm across; florets all strap-like, above longer, slender-pointed, green bracts; flowerheads borne on swollen stalk tips **Blooms:** May to August **Fruits:** ribbed, seed-like achenes 2.5–3.5 cm long, with a stout beak supporting a parachute of feathery white hairs **Habitat:** open, disturbed sites **Distribution:** Europe; naturalized from Newfoundland to Alaska to Texas **Pick:** freely

Annual Sunflower

Helianthus annuus

Annual sunflower was one of the first plants cultivated in North America. Its oily seeds were usually roasted, shelled and ground into meal for making gruel or bread. Often this meal was mixed with fat and formed into flat cakes. Today, sunflower seeds are popular in breads, cereals, salads and countless other dishes. Although we generally think of only the seeds as edible, the bright yellow strap-like florets make a colourful salad garnish. The leaves and immature flowerheads provide a vegetable with an artichoke-like flavour. In the 1600s, they were reputed to equal artichokes in flavour and surpass them in procuring bodily lust. • The name *Helianthus*, 'sun flower,' refers to the fact that the flowerheads constantly turn to face the sun.

Plant: coarse, rough-hairy annual plant 50–300 cm tall **Leaves:** mostly alternate, ovate to heart-shaped, 6–25 cm long, usually toothed and stalked
Flowerheads: yellow, 5–15 cm across; many strap-like florets surrounding a 3–4 cm, red-brown button of tubular florets, with broad, abruptly slender-pointed bracts at the base; 1 to few flowerheads **Blooms:** July to September
Fruits: 2–4-sided, seed-like achenes 5–10 mm long, containing a white seed
Habitat: moist, disturbed sites
Distribution: native in the western U.S.; naturalized across North America and around the world **Pick:** freely

Great Blanketflower

Gaillardia aristata

As its common name suggests, this vibrant wildflower displays the bold colours of blankets from the American Southwest. Blanketflower can last for days as a cut flower. It is also a beautiful, hardy plant for wildflower gardens, easily grown from seed or by transplanting leafy (not blooming) plants. Many showy cultivars have been developed. • Blanketflower plants have been boiled to make teas for problems ranging from headaches to tuberculosis and cancer. Sometimes, great blanketflower was used to predict a patient's future. When plants were boiled for a long time and the water remained clear or whitish, the person would die. A reddish or well-coloured liquid indicated that the patient would recover. • Great blanketflower has also been called great-flowered gaillardia.

Plant: greyish-hairy perennial 20–70 cm tall, from slender taproot **Leaves:** oblong to lance-shaped, 5–15 cm long, smooth-edged to deeply lobed **Flowerheads:** yellow with a purplish centre, 3–7 cm across, with 6–18 broad, yellow (often purple-based), 3-lobed strap-like florets around a domed 1–4 cm button of purplish tubular florets; flowerheads long-stalked, 1 to several
Blooms: May to September **Fruits:** 3-sided, seed-like achenes, tipped with 5–10 papery scales **Habitat:** dry, open sites **Distribution:** native from Manitoba to B.C. to New Mexico; occasionally naturalized elsewhere
Pick: a few

Prairie Coneflower

Ratibida columnifera

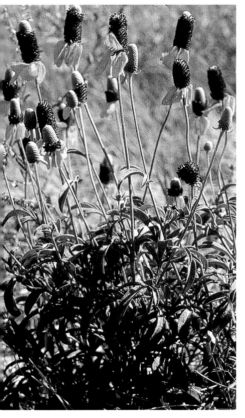

The distinctive heads of this native plant are unmistakable. 'Coneflower' refers to the tall cone of tubular florets at the centre of each flowerhead. Another common name, red-spike Mexican-hat, likens the ring of strap-like florets to the brim of a Mexican hat, with a high, cylindrical hat crown. • Many tribes used fragrant prairie coneflower leaves to make a pleasant tea. The flower cones are said to be edible, dried or semidried, with a flavour like corn. The younger the cone, the better the taste, but all are quite chewy and can take some time to munch. • In dry regions, this hardy wildflower adorns roadsides, parks, recreation areas and prairie restoration sites. It makes a wonderful addition to prairie gardens as well. • Prairie coneflower has also been called long-headed coneflower.

Plant: erect perennial 30–70 cm tall, with stiff, grooved stems branched near the base; from taproot **Leaves:** hairy, pinnately divided into 5–9 slender lobes
Flowerheads: yellow to almost orange (rarely purplish), with spreading to backward-bending strap-like florets 1.5–2.5 cm long, around a 1–4 cm long cylinder of grey to yellow to purple-brown tubular florets; flowerheads long-stalked, few to many
Blooms: June to September
Fruits: grey-black, seed-like achenes 2 mm long **Habitat:** dry, open, often disturbed sites **Distribution:** native from Ontario to B.C. to the southern U.S.; occasionally introduced **Pick:** a few

Hairy False-Golden-Aster

Heterotheca villosa

This hardy little wildflower thrives in dry, sunny sites, so it does well in prairie gardens without extra watering. Seed is commercially available, or it can be collected from September to October. • Some tribes boiled the fuzzy plants to make a soothing medicinal tea for aiding sleep. The same tea was used as a wash for healing bruises and reducing swelling in the legs. For toothaches, a heated root was applied to ease the pain. • The name *Heterotheca* comes from the Greek *heteros*, 'different,' and *theca*, 'container,' because the seed-like fruits of the outer, strap-like florets are different from those produced by the inner, tubular florets. The species name, *villosa*, means 'shaggy-haired.' • *H. villosa* has also been called *Chrysopsis villosa*, a name taken from the Greek *chrysos*, 'gold,' and *opsis*, 'aspect' or 'face.'

Plant: grey-green, silky-hairy perennial 10–60 cm tall, sometimes glandular, with clumped stems from woody-crowned taproot **Leaves:** numerous, elliptic to oblong, 2–5 cm long **Flowerheads:** yellow, about 2.5 cm across, with 10–25 strap-like florets around a yellow button of tubular florets, each head with overlapping rows of bracts at the base; 1 to several flowerheads in flat-topped clusters **Blooms:** July to September **Fruits:** hairy, flattened, seed-like achenes tipped with a parachute of silky white hairs **Habitat:** dry, open sites **Distribution:** native from Ontario to B.C., south through the U.S. **Pick:** a few

Curly-Cup Gumweed

Grindelia squarrosa

The fragrance of curly-cup gumweed is strongest on hot, sunny days. Like a number of other resinous plants, gumweed has provided many medicines. Its upper stems and leaves were brewed to make teas for coughs, asthma, bronchitis, indigestion and kidney or bladder problems. The sticky flowerheads were pounded or boiled to make poultices or washes for wounds, burns, sores, pimples and poison-ivy rashes. Several patents have been granted for gumweed substances, and the essential oil is in demand for aromatherapy. • Curly-cup gumweed is easily recognized by the gummy, strongly hooked bracts on its flowerheads. The name *squarrosa* means 'rough with outward-projecting tips,' a reference to these bracts.

Plant: aromatic biennial or short-lived perennial 30–60 cm tall, with much-branched stems from taproot **Leaves:** dotted with resin glands, oblong, 1–4 cm long, irregularly toothed or lobed, clasping the stem **Flowerheads:** yellow, 2–3 cm across, with 25–40 strap-like florets around a broad button of tubular florets and with overlapping rows of sticky, backward-curling bracts at the base; numerous flowerheads in flat-topped clusters **Blooms:** July to September **Fruits:** 4–5-ribbed, seed-like achenes, tipped with a few slender bristles (soon shed) **Habitat:** dry, open sites **Distribution:** Newfoundland to B.C., south through the U.S. **Pick:** a few

Oxeye Daisy

Leucanthemum vulgare

This highly successful weed originated in Asia and spread into Europe hundreds of years ago. First introduced to eastern North America in the early 1600s, it is now one of the most common wildflowers across the continent. Many travellers enjoy the cheerful blooms, which fill ditches and blanket fields, but farmers view oxeye daisy as an aggressive weed that rapidly replaces valuable forage plants. • Daisies have long been part of European lore, twisted into daisy chains and circlets at picnics and school commencements, or plucked of their white 'petals' (really strap-like florets) to the chant 'He loves me, he loves me not.' • This species previously had a lovely rhyming name, *Chrysanthemum leucanthemum*.

Plant: slender, erect perennial 20–90 cm tall, from spreading rootstock **Leaves:** basal and alternate, 4–15 cm long, coarsely toothed or lobed, smaller and stalkless upwards
Flowerheads: white, 2.5–5 cm across; 15–35 strap-like florets around a bright yellow, 1–2 cm button of tubular florets, with dry, brown-edged bracts at the base; flowerheads single
Blooms: May to September **Fruits:** 10-ribbed, seed-like achenes **Habitat:** open, disturbed sites **Distribution:** Eurasia; naturalized from Newfoundland to Alaska to Texas **Pick:** freely

Scentless Chamomile

Tripleurospermum perforata

An aggressive invader of pastures and hay fields, scentless chamomile is quick to infest cropland. Today, this flourishing immigrant is classified as a noxious weed across western Canada and in Quebec. One plant can produce more than 300,000 seeds, which may remain dormant for several years, waiting until the time is right to germinate and produce a whole new generation of plants. • At first glance, this species could be mistaken for oxeye daisy (p. 79), but upon closer examination, the finely divided leaves will clearly identify scentless chamomile. This plant is also very similar to its well-known but sweetly scented relative, wild chamomile *(Matricaria recutita)*. A tea from that fragrant species has been used for centuries as a pleasant-tasting drink and as a medicine. • *T. perforata* has also been called *Matricaria perforata* and *M. maritima* (in part).

Plant: erect, nearly scentless annual (usually), biennial or short-lived perennial 10–70 cm tall
Leaves: 2–8 cm long, pinnately divided into slender, often thread-like parts
Flowerheads: white, 2.5–5 cm across; 12–25 strap-like florets around a bright yellow, 8–15 mm hemisphere of tubular florets; several to many flowerheads **Blooms:** July to September **Fruits:** rectangular, 3-ribbed, seed-like achenes **Habitat:** open, disturbed sites **Distribution:** Eurasia; naturalized from Newfoundland to Alaska to the central U.S.
Pick: freely

Showy Wood-Aster

Eurybia conspicua

Although the violet blue blooms of showy wood-aster do not appear until late summer or autumn, the plant is uniquely fragrant early in the year. If you rub your fingers over its rough, sandpapery leaves in springtime, you will come away with a wonderful citrus-like perfume. Livestock are also said to enjoy this sweet-scented plant. • Showy wood-aster was not widely used by Native peoples, but some tribes used its large leaves as poultices on boils or soaked the roots in water to make medicinal washes for healing sores and boils. • As you might suspect, the epithet *conspicua* means 'conspicuous,' and these stately plants with their showy flower clusters are certainly hard to miss. This species has also been called showy aster and *Aster conspicuus*.

Plant: coarse, stiff-hairy perennial 30–90 cm tall, with erect stems from strong, creeping rootstock **Leaves:** elliptic to ovate, 6–15 cm long, sharply toothed, usually stalkless and clasping; mature leaves firm and sandpapery above **Flowerheads:** violet blue, about 2–3 cm across, with 12–35 strap-like florets around a yellow button of tubular florets; basal bracts green-tipped, glandular, in 5 overlapping rows; few to many flowerheads in flat-topped to rounded clusters
Blooms: July to October **Fruits:** hairless, veined, seed-like achenes tipped with a cluster of silky white hairs **Habitat:** open, moist to dry sites **Distribution:** native from Manitoba to B.C. to Wyoming **Pick:** a few

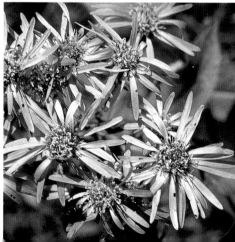

Fringed American-Aster

Symphyotrichum ciliolatum

This cheerful blue wildflower brightens waysides long after most other blossoms have faded. Many different aster-like plants grow wild in Alberta, but fringed American-aster is one of the easiest to identify. It has distinctive heart-shaped lower leaves with long, fringed stalks. • Native peoples sometimes used this plant for medicine. They boiled the strongly scented roots to make eye drops, and they used the smoke from burning roots to revive people who had fainted in sweat baths. Sometimes a paper cone was used to force the smoke up the nose of an unconscious patient. • The specific epithet *ciliolatum* means 'fringed,' a reference to the hairy-edged leaf stalks. *S. ciliolatum* has also been called *Aster ciliolatus*, fringed aster and Lindley's aster.

Plant: erect perennial 20–120 cm tall, from spreading rootstock **Leaves:** 4–12 cm long, pointed; lowest leaves toothed, heart-shaped, with notched bases and slender, hairy-edged stalks; stem leaves lance-shaped, usually stalkless **Flowerheads:** pale blue to purplish, 1.5–3 cm across; 12–25 strap-like florets around a button of yellow tubular florets, with slender bracts at the base; flowerheads in branched, open clusters **Blooms:** July to October **Fruits:** seed-like achenes tipped with a parachute of silky white hairs **Habitat:** woodlands and open, often disturbed sites **Distribution:** native from Quebec to B.C., south to the northern U.S. **Pick:** a few

Smooth Blue American-Aster

Symphyotrichum laeve

Smooth blue American-aster is one of the most common asters in western Canada. In autumn, the showy flowers produce beautiful banks of blue, long after most other wildflowers have faded. This showy plant has great potential as a garden subject, and it is easily grown from rootstock cuttings or from seed (either collected from the wild or produced commercially). • Some tribes used smooth blue American-aster for medicine. Teething babies were given the roots to chew, and people packed rootstock fragments into cavities to relieve toothaches. • 'Aster,' the Greek word for 'star,' refers to the star-shaped flowers. According to ancient legend, asters were created by a god scattering stardust over the landscape. The specific epithet *laeve*, 'smooth,' refers to the hairless plant. *S. laeve* has also been called *Aster laevis* and smooth blue aster.

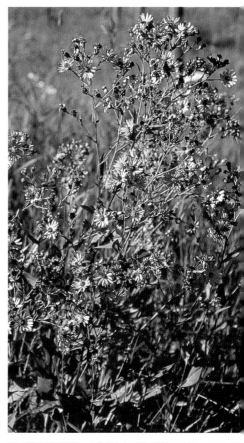

Plant: erect, hairless, often blue-green perennial 30–120 cm tall, from rootstock **Leaves:** thick, oval to oblong, 2–10 cm long, with winged stalks; upper leaves stalk-less, often clasping **Flowerheads:** pale blue to dark purple, 2–3 cm across, with 20 or more strap-like florets around a yellow button of tubular florets and with firm, overlapping bracts at the base; few to many flowerheads in open clusters **Blooms:** July to September **Fruits:** hairless, seed-like achenes tipped with tawny, hair-like bristles **Habitat:** open sites **Distribution:** native from Quebec to the Yukon to Texas **Pick:** a few

Smooth Fleabane

Erigeron glabellus

These showy blue flowerheads make a lovely addition to wildflower gardens. Smooth fleabane usually produces large quantities of seed with good germination, and it can also be grown by dividing mature plants in spring or fall. • It is often difficult to distinguish fleabanes (*Erigeron* species) from asters (*Aster, Eurybia* and *Symphyotrichum* species, pp. 81–83). As a general rule, fleabanes flower earlier than asters, and the strap-like florets of fleabanes are more slender and numerous than those encircling an aster flowerhead. • Fleabane leaves were sometimes used to make salves for relieving pain and swelling. • The name *Erigeron* comes from the Greek *eri,* 'early,' and *geron,* 'old man,' because the flowers appear early in the year and soon produce fluffy grey seed clusters resembling small, grey-haired heads.

Plant: biennial or perennial 10–50 cm tall, from fibrous roots **Leaves:** usually stiff-hairy, widest above the middle, 5–15 cm long; upper leaves smaller and stalkless **Flowerheads:** blue, pink or whitish, 1–2 cm across, with 125–175 slender (up to 1 mm wide) strap-like florets around a button of yellow tubular florets and with slender, hairy bracts at the base; usually 1–3 flowerheads (sometimes up to 10) **Blooms:** June to August **Fruits:** seed-like achenes with a tuft of white to reddish hairs **Habitat:** open sites **Distribution:** native from Ontario to Alaska, south to New Mexico **Pick:** a few

Philadelphia Fleabane

Erigeron philadelphicus

Philadelphia fleabane is usually considered a weed to be pulled on sight in gardens and along sidewalks. However, if left to grow, this pretty native wildflower will produce lovely flowerheads—each ringed with more than 100 slender florets—from late spring to autumn. • In the early 1900s, physicians used oils from the leaves and flower clusters of this plant to speed up contractions and to stop bleeding during births. Philadelphia fleabane has also been used to help control nosebleeds and internal bleeding and to treat bad coughs, fevers and even diabetes and tumours. • The smoke produced by burning some *Erigeron* species was used to drive away fleas and other insect pests, giving rise to the common name fleabane.

Plant: soft-hairy biennial or perennial 15–90 cm tall, from rootstock and runners **Leaves:** blunt-toothed to lobed, 5–15 cm long; lower leaves short-stalked, stem leaves stalkless and clasping **Flowerheads:** rose purple to white, 1–2.5 cm across, with 100–400 slender strap-like florets around a yellow button of tubular florets; flowerheads in branched clusters **Blooms:** April to August **Fruits:** seed-like achenes tipped with a tuft of white hairs
Habitat: various; usually disturbed sites
Distribution: native from Newfoundland to the Yukon to Texas **Pick:** a few

Marsh Ragwort

Senecio congestus

In dry years, vivid yellow skirts of marsh ragwort often ring prairie sloughs and ponds. Usually, these large, hairy plants (also appropriately called woolly-mammoth plant) shoot up to their full height and produce flowers and seeds in a few short weeks. Sometimes frost will kill the flowers, and the plants grow again the following year. • Although young plants have occasionally been added to salads or cooked in soups and stews, marsh ragwort should be treated with caution. Some western Inuit believed that its roots were poisonous, and of the nearly 50 species of *Senecio* in North America, 7 are suspected or proven to be toxic. Also, marsh ragwort produces large amounts of highly allergenic pollen; hay fever sufferers beware! • The epithet *congestus* refers to the compact (congested) flower clusters, not to this plant's effect on susceptible noses.

Plant: erect annual (occasionally biennial) 20–100 cm tall, with hollow stems from fibrous roots **Leaves:** 5–15 cm long, wavy-edged **Flowerheads:** yellow, 1–2 cm across, with short strap-like florets around a button of tubular florets and with overlapping, hairy bracts at the base; flowerheads in rounded to flat-topped clusters **Blooms:** June to August **Fruits:** seed-like achenes, tipped with tufted white hairs **Habitat:** open sites near water **Distribution:** native from Newfoundland to Alaska to the north-central U.S., and around the world **Pick:** a few; caution

Arctic Sweet-Colt's-Foot

Petasites frigidus

This feathery white wildflower is one of our first signs of spring. It's hard to believe that such a pretty little plant could cause any trouble, but it has. Sweet-colt's-foot plants are rich in minerals, and their ashes were sometimes used as a salt substitute. In some parts of the southwestern U.S., where salt supplies were limited, control of sweet-colt's-foot colonies sparked rivalries intense enough that battles sometimes ensued. • Sweet-colt's-foot can provide more than just salt. Its leaves and flowering stems, though fuzzy, have been eaten steamed, stir-fried and boiled. The flower clusters can be fried in batter or chopped and tossed into casseroles or soups. *Note:* Pregnant women should not eat this plant or drink sweet-colt's-foot tea. • This widespread, complex species now includes *P. palmatus*, *P. sagittatus*, *P. hyperboreus* and *P. nivalis*. The variety *sagittatus* is shown here.

Plant: erect perennial 10–50 cm tall, from creeping rootstock **Leaves:** basal, 10–30 cm long, arrowhead-shaped and shallowly toothed to smooth-edged, or round to triangular and deeply lobed, white-woolly underneath **Flowerheads:** whitish, about 8 mm across, with few strap-like florets around a cluster of tubular florets; flowerheads in rounded, elongating clusters **Blooms:** May **Fruits:** seed-like achenes with silky hairs, forming fluffy, white heads 2–3.5 cm long **Habitat:** moist to wet sites **Distribution:** native from Labrador to Alaska to Colorado **Pick:** none

Common Tansy

Tanacetum vulgare

Common tansy was one of the first medicinal herbs brought to North America. Traditionally it was used to repel lice and fleas, kill intestinal worms and induce abortions, sometimes with fatal results for mother and child. It has also been used to flavour liqueurs, cakes, puddings, omelettes, salads and cheeses, but now we know it should never be used in food unless its toxins (especially thujone) have been removed. • Common tansy was the herb that made Ganymede, beautiful cup-bearer of the Greek gods, immortal. For that reason, and because of its strong, insect-repelling fragrance, this plant was used to preserve bodies in ancient Greece. • In Canada, common tansy is a troublesome weed. One plant can produce more than 50,000 seeds, and established plants spread rapidly by creeping rootstocks.

Plant: coarse, leafy, aromatic perennial 40–100 cm tall **Leaves:** dotted with glands, 10–20 cm long, pinnately divided into deeply lobed and/or sharply toothed leaflets; short-stalked to stalkless **Flowerheads:** deep yellow, 5–10 mm across; florets all tubular; flowerheads in flat-topped clusters of 20–200 **Blooms:** July to September **Fruits:** 5-ribbed, seed-like achenes **Habitat:** disturbed sites **Distribution:** Eurasia; naturalized across most of North America **Pick:** freely

Pineappleweed

Matricaria discoidea

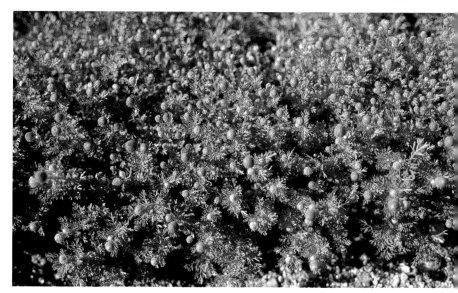

This aromatic herb is closely related to chamomile (*M. recutita;* see p. 80) and has been used in many of the same ways. Bruised pineappleweed smells like freshly cut pineapple. The fragrant plants make an excellent deodorant, capable of masking even the strong smell of fish when rubbed on hands. Pineappleweed can also be hung as an air freshener, stuffed into pillows and sachets, dropped into hot bath water for an aromatic soak, or rubbed over skin or clothing as perfume and insect repellent. The flower-heads can be nibbled straight from the plant, tossed into salads as a lemony garnish or steeped in water to make a fragrant tea. The tea acts as a mild sedative for inducing sleep and soothing upset stomachs. • *M. discoidea* has also been called *M. matricarioides.*

Plant: leafy, low-branching annual 5–40 cm tall
Leaves: 1–5 cm long, 2–3 times pinnately divided into slender, sometimes thread-like parts **Flowerheads:** yellow, 5–9 mm across, cone-shaped; florets all tubular, above dry, thin-edged bracts; several to many flowerheads
Blooms: May to September **Fruits:** 2-ribbed, often 5-sided, seed-like achenes
Habitat: open, disturbed sites
Distribution: native in the western cordillera; naturalized across most of North America
Pick: freely

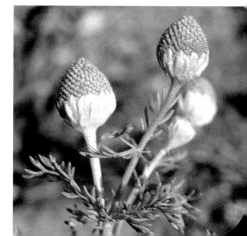

Rosy Pussytoes

Antennaria rosea

These small, fuzzy plants were not commonly used by Native peoples, but the leaves were sometimes chewed for pleasure, especially by children, or were added to smoking mixtures. Some tribes soaked dried plants with hot water and then applied the wet mass to the eyes to soothe snow blindness. • Rosy pussytoes has been called rosy everlasting because the dried flowers keep their colour for many months. These blooms make a pretty addition to dried-flower arrangements. • Each plant produces either male or female flowers, but male plants are rarely found. Fortunately, pussytoes can produce seed without fertilization. Doing so helps the plants spread rapidly but also creates confusion in classification. Over the years, three of our most common pussytoes— little-leaved *(A. parvifolia)*, small-leaved *(A. microphylla)* and rosy *(A. rosea)*—have been variously classified as the same species.

Plant: tufted to mat-forming perennial 5–40 cm tall, with leafy, creeping stems
Leaves: densely white- or grey-woolly on both sides, mainly basal, spatula-shaped, 1–2.5 cm long; stem leaves 7–12, slender
Flowerheads: pinkish; florets all tubular, above a 4–7 mm high cluster of pink-tipped bracts; flowerheads in compact, rounded clusters **Blooms:** May to August
Fruits: seed-like achenes, tipped with a tuft of white hairs **Habitat:** dry, open sites
Distribution: native from Newfoundland to Alaska, south through the western U.S.; rare in Quebec and Ontario **Pick:** a few

Common Yarrow

Achillea millefolium

In the Middle Ages, common yarrow was found in every monastery, apothecary shop and household medicine chest, ready to treat anyone who admitted to illness. It was used most often to stimulate sweating, reduce inflammation and stop bleeding.
• The fresh, young leaves also furnished a rather bitter, aromatic salad green. When eaten today, the young leaves are often cooked as a vegetable or potherb, and the older leaves provide a sage-like seasoning or a nourishing tea. Housewives and wild birds alike have used this pungent plant to repel fleas and other insects. Smoke from burning yarrow flowers was said to repel both insects and evil spirits, and smouldering seed heads were used to keep witches at bay.

Plant: aromatic perennial 20–100 cm tall, from spreading rootstock
Leaves: feathery, 3–15 cm long, finely divided, often grey-hairy
Flowerheads: white to pink, 5–6 mm across; 4–6 short strap-like florets around 10–30 yellow tubular florets above overlapping, dark-edged bracts; flowerheads in flat-topped clusters 2–10 cm wide **Blooms:** June to September **Fruits:** hairless, flattened, seed-like achenes **Habitat:** highly variable; often disturbed sites
Distribution: native throughout North America and around the world
Pick: a few

Spike-Like Goldenrod

Solidago simplex

The name *Solidago*, from the Latin *solidus*, 'whole,' and *ago*, 'to do or make,' refers to the alleged healing properties of goldenrods. Some tribes boiled the resinous, aromatic plants of spike-like goldenrod to make medicinal teas for improving appetite and treating syphilis. The leaves were also toasted, powdered and combined with grease to make a poultice for treating mumps.

• Goldenrod blossoms are recommended for use in hair rinses (for blondes), facial steams and herbal baths. In the kitchen, goldenrod leaves and flowers have been cooked as potherbs and used in teas, and the seeds have been used to thicken soups. The flowers also add colour to breads and pancakes.

• This species has sometimes been called *S. spathulata*, *S. decumbens* and mountain goldenrod.

Plant: erect perennial 10–50 cm tall, from branched rootstock **Leaves:** mainly basal, tongue-shaped, 2–10 cm long, with a few shallow, rounded teeth towards the tip **Flowerheads:** yellow, about 8 mm high, with 7–10 strap-like florets around a clump of about 13 tubular florets; bracts blunt-tipped, often sticky, in a cluster 4–6 mm high; flowerheads forming dense, narrow clusters **Blooms:** late July to September **Fruits:** seed-like achenes 2 mm long, tipped with silky white hairs **Habitat:** dry, open sites **Distribution:** native from Nova Scotia to Alaska, south through the U.S. **Pick:** a few

Canada Goldenrod

Solidago canadensis

This eye-catching native wildflower has been much maligned as the guilty party in countless hay fever attacks. In fact, goldenrod pollen is too heavy to travel on the wind; insects must carry it. The real hay fever culprits are inconspicuous plants, such as ragweeds (*Ambrosia* species), that flower at the same time. Plants with wind-pollinated flowers often go unnoticed because they don't have showy blooms. • Some large goldenrod colonies are estimated to be about 100 years old. Older, central plants may eventually die back, creating a ring, but usually colonies are too dense for other plants to invade. • Beautiful Canada goldenrod, also known as graceful goldenrod, is seldom grown in its native land, but it is said to be a popular subject in European gardens.

Plant: perennial 25–100 cm tall with finely hairy upper stems, from spreading rootstock
Leaves: 3–15 cm long, 5–20 mm wide, toothed, finely hairy underneath (at least on main veins), stalk-less **Flowerheads:** yellow, 2–4 mm across; 10–17 strap-like florets and 2–8 tubular florets above overlapping, green-tipped bracts; flowerheads on 1-sided branches in pyramidal clusters **Blooms:** August to October **Fruits:** seed-like achenes tipped with tufted white hairs **Habitat:** open sites **Distribution:** native from Newfoundland to Alaska to Texas **Pick:** a few

Leafy Spurge
Euphorbia esula

This aggressive weed appeared in Ontario in 1889. A mere 40 years later it had spread to British Columbia, and within a century more than 1 million hectares had become infested in North America. With their exploding capsules, leafy spurge plants can shoot seeds up to 5 m away. The seeds also float along streams to establish new colonies. To make matters worse, tiny pieces of the deep, easily broken roots can grow into new plants, and the decaying leaves poison livestock (though sheep seem to be immune). Leafy spurge quickly crowds out native plants and reduces rangeland productivity by 50–75%. • The name *Euphorbia* honours Euphorbus, physician to a king of Mauritania in the first century BC. • Take care! The milky juice can burn sensitive skin and may cause blindness if it touches the eyes.

Plant: hairless perennial 30–70 cm tall, from strong, spreading roots **Leaves:** slender, 3–8 cm long, stalkless **Flowers:** tiny, in 2 mm wide groups resembling single flowers; each group has 4 male flowers and 1 stalked female flower in a cup with 4 crescent-shaped glands above 2 petal-like bracts; flower groups in branched, umbrella-shaped clusters with circles (whorls) of leaves at the main base and paired, heart-shaped bracts below smaller sub-clusters **Blooms:** June to August **Fruits:** 3–3.5 mm capsules **Habitat:** disturbed sites **Distribution:** Eurasia; naturalized across temperate North America **Pick:** freely; caution

Heart-Leaved Alexanders

Zizia aptera

Many members of the carrot family (pp. 95–98) have fascinating histories. This widespread wildflower, by contrast, seems to have been largely overlooked by people. The young flower clusters of some *Zizia* species are reportedly added to salads occasionally, but the most common use for heart-leaved Alexanders has been in gardens. A hardy perennial, it can tolerate alkaline soils and cold winters, but it needs sun and consistently moist soil to really thrive. Beds where heart-leaved Alexanders is planted should not dry out between waterings. Most gardeners appreciate the attractive, early flowers and the interesting form and texture of the leaves. Seed is commercially available, but it requires a long period of cold treatment to germinate successfully. • The name *Zizia* commemorates Johann Baptist Ziz, a German botanist who lived from 1779 to 1829. *Aptera* means 'wingless,' a reference to the fruits. Heart-leaved Alexanders has also been called heart-leaved meadow-parsnip.

Plant: hairless, shiny perennial 20–60 cm tall, from cluster of fleshy roots **Leaves:** mainly basal, heart-shaped, finely toothed, 2–10 cm long, with long stalks; the few stem leaves, once or twice divided in threes, with broad, toothed leaflets **Flowers:** bright yellow, tiny; many in repeatedly divided, umbrella-shaped clusters 2.5–5 cm across **Blooms:** May to July **Fruits:** hairless, narrowly ribbed, seed-like schizocarps 2–4 mm long **Habitat:** moist meadows and prairies **Distribution:** native from Quebec to B.C. to Florida and Nevada **Pick:** a few

Common Cow-Parsnip

Heracleum maximum

Although mature cow-parsnip is strong-smelling, many tribes used it for food. Young shoots and stems were peeled, then cooked or eaten raw, often dipped in grease or sugar. Sometimes stalks were roasted in coals and then peeled. The aromatic seeds flavoured soups and stews, and the ashes of burned leaves became a kind of salt. Some people liken the roots to rutabagas, but others find the taste too strong to be enjoyable. • The dried, hollow stems can be used to make elk and moose whistles, children's flutes, drinking straws and toy blowguns, but these items may irritate the lips. People with sensitive skin often develop rashes when contact with cow-parsnip is followed by exposure to bright sunlight. It is a good idea to gather this robust plant with gloves. • *H. maximum* has also been called *H. lanatum*.

Plant: hairy perennial 1–3 m tall, with hollow stems **Leaves:** divided into 3 large (10–30 cm), lobed, toothed leaflets; upper leaf stalks with enlarged bases **Flowers:** small, white; many in twice-divided, umbrella-like clusters 10–20 cm wide, with 15–30 main branches **Blooms:** June to July **Fruits:** flattened, heart-shaped, seed-like schizocarps 8–12 mm long **Habitat:** moist, rich sites **Distribution:** native across North America and in Siberia **Pick:** a few; caution

Common Water-Parsnip

Sium suave

Some tribes believed the smoke from common water-parsnip seeds could drive away evil spirits trying to steal a hunter's luck. The slender, fleshy, nutty-flavoured roots were harvested in early spring and eaten raw or cooked. The leaves are also said to be edible but very strong-tasting. However, water-parsnip looks so similar to its highly poisonous relatives (such as spotted water-hemlock, p. 98), it is better left alone. Reports of poisoning most likely come from confusion with toxic species. Water-parsnip has ribbed stems and a circle (whorl) of small bracts at the base of each of its flower clusters; water-hemlock has smooth, rounded stalks and usually lacks bracts. Unfortunately, by the time the water-parsnip is large enough to identify with certainty, its roots are too woody to eat.

Plant: erect perennial 60–200 cm tall, from fibrous roots **Leaves:** pinnately divided into 7–17 narrow, sharply toothed leaflets 5–10 cm long **Flowers:** tiny, white; many in flat-topped, 3–12 cm wide, umbrella-shaped clusters with 6–20 main branches above a ring of 5–8 slender bracts **Blooms:** July to September **Fruits:** oval, corky-ribbed, seed-like schizocarps 2–3 mm long **Habitat:** wet, open sites **Distribution:** native from Newfoundland to Alaska to the southern U.S. and in Siberia **Pick:** none

Spotted Water-Hemlock
Cicuta maculata

One night during his famous western expedition (1857–60), John Palliser heard strange noises coming from a wetland. His Métis guides told him the sounds came from the powerful, deadly water-hemlocks that lurked in the swamp. • Spotted water-hemlock is one of our most poisonous wild plants: a single rootstock can kill a horse. Children have been poisoned by using peashooters made from the stems. Symptoms include stomach pains, vomiting, weak and rapid pulse and convulsions. If you think someone might have eaten any part of a water-hemlock, take a sample from the plant and get medical help right away. • Spotted water-hemlock is distinguished by its swollen, chambered rootstocks and yellowish, oily, foul-smelling sap. Also, the main side-veins of the leaves end at the bases of the leaf teeth, and not at the tooth tips. Remember: 'Vein to the cut, pain in the gut!'

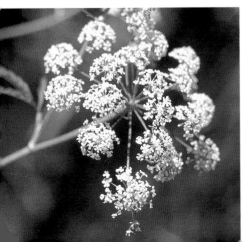

Plant: erect perennial 60–200 cm tall, with thick-based stems from fibrous roots
Leaves: 2–3 times pinnately divided into sharply toothed leaflets 3–10 cm long
Flowers: tiny, white; many in 5–12 cm wide, umbrella-shaped clusters, usually without bracts at the base **Blooms:** June to August **Fruits:** round, slightly flattened, corky-ribbed, seed-like schizocarps 2–4 mm long **Habitat:** wet sites
Distribution: native from Nova Scotia to Alaska to Mexico **Pick:** none (abundant, but very toxic)

False-Toadflax

Comandra umbellata

This delicate white flower makes a pretty addition to wildflower gardens. Its innocent appearance, however, belies a sinister side. False-toadflax always grows best near other plants because it locks onto the roots of its neighbours to steal water and nutrients. Many different plants can be hosts for this parasite.
• The fully grown, slightly green fruits are edible, but they are rarely abundant enough to provide more than a nibble. This scarcity is probably for the best, because too many cause nausea, and false-toadflax is known to accumulate toxic levels of selenium when this element occurs in the soil. Some people find the oily drupes sweet and delicious, while others consider them bland. The ripe, brown fruits are also said to be edible, but less flavourful.
• The leaves and stems have been thought to resemble those of toad-flax (butter-and-eggs, p. 38), hence the common names false-toadflax and bastard-toadflax.

Plant: erect, blue-green perennial 10–30 cm tall, in clumps and colonies from creeping rootstock **Leaves:** firm, slender, 1–3 cm long, essentially stalkless **Flowers:** greenish white to pinkish, 3–5 mm across, with 5 pointed, petal-like sepals; flowers numerous, in groups of 3–5 in larger, ovoid clusters **Blooms:** May to July **Fruits:** firm, brownish green drupes, 4–8 mm long, tipped with old sepals **Habitat:** gravelly, open slopes **Distribution:** native from Newfoundland to the Yukon to the southern U.S. **Pick:** a few

Slender Blue Beardtongue

Penstemon procerus

Slender blue beardtongue often forms large colonies, and it makes a lovely addition to wildflower gardens. It is easily grown from seed, but cold treatment of the seeds is important, increasing germination rates from about 5% to over 50%. • Some tribes boiled the plants to make a tea that cleansed the system by causing vomiting and diarrhea. Dark-roasted stems and leaves were powdered and sprinkled on skin to heal sores, rashes and other irritations. Modern-day herbalists recommend oils infused with beardtongue as an ingredient in soothing salves and ointments. • *Penstemon* is from the Greek *pente*, 'five,' and *stemon*, 'thread,' in reference to the slender, sterile fifth stamen in each flower. Although this beardtongue is not especially large, its specific epithet, *procerus*, means 'very tall.' • Slender blue beardtongue has also been called pincushion beardtongue.

Plant: slender, erect perennial 15–40 cm tall, from branched rootstock **Leaves:** paired, hairless, lance-shaped, usually widest above midleaf, 2.5–8 cm long, smooth-edged **Flowers:** purplish blue (rarely pinkish or white), trumpet-shaped, 6–11 mm long, weakly 2-lipped with 2 upper and 3 lower petal lobes; flowers whorled in dense, sometimes interrupted spikes **Blooms:** June to August **Fruits:** egg-shaped capsules 2–3 mm long, containing many angular seeds **Habitat:** moist, open sites **Distribution:** native from Manitoba to Alaska to California **Pick:** a few

Blue Giant-Hyssop
Agastache foeniculum

This tall, leafy plant, with its pleasant anise-like fragrance, has often been used for food and medicine. Young plants provide cooked greens and flavouring for soups and stews. The fresh flowers add splashes of purple to salads and cooked dishes. Fresh or dried leaves, covered with boiling water and steeped or simmered, produce a delicately licorice-flavoured tea. The leaves also add flavour to commercial teas. Cooled giant-hyssop leaf tea is still drunk occasionally to relieve coughs and chest pains. It has been credited with curing dispirited hearts and inducing sweating. • This robust, common mint could prove to be a source of essential oil for perfume and aromatherapy. It is easily grown from seeds, cuttings or root divisions, particularly on sandy, limy, well-drained soil in sunny sites. The flower clusters dry well and look beautiful in dried floral arrangements.

Plant: erect perennial 30–100 cm tall, with 4-sided stems from creeping rootstock
Leaves: paired, whitish underneath with fine, close hairs, ovate, 2–7 cm long, coarsely toothed, short-stalked
Flowers: blue, funnel-shaped, 2-lipped, 6–12 mm long, with a blue, hairy, 5-lobed calyx; flowers in dense, usually interrupted spikes 2–10 cm long **Blooms:** July to August **Fruits:** 4 small nutlets within the calyx **Habitat:** well-drained, open sites **Distribution:** native from Quebec to Alberta to the central U.S. **Pick:** a few

Wild Mint

Mentha arvensis

Widespread but inconspicuous, this species is often discovered by smell rather than by sight. Bruised plants give off a strong minty fragrance announcing their presence. • Like its domesticated European cousins spearmint *(M. spicata)* and peppermint *(M. piperata)*, wild mint has been used for centuries as food and medicine. Plants can be cooked as greens, added to stews or used to flavour meat dishes, salads and jellies. Sometimes the fragrant powdered leaves were sprinkled over drying fruit or meat to repel insects. Most commonly, wild mint has been brewed into tea, a pleasant beverage that has also been used to treat colds, coughs, fevers, indigestion, vomiting, kidney problems, headaches and even the effects of being caught in a whirlwind. Menthol, the essential oil in mint, has been shown to relieve pain and control vomiting. • Mints have also been used to freshen air and to mask human scent on animal traps.

Plant: aromatic perennial 20–80 cm tall, dotted with tiny glands, with 4-sided stems from spreading rootstock **Leaves:** paired, lance- to egg-shaped, 2–8 cm long, toothed **Flowers:** pale purple to pink or whitish, funnel-shaped, 4–7 mm long, with 4–5 spreading petal lobes; flowers whorled in upper leaf axils **Blooms:** July to September **Fruits:** 4 small, egg-shaped nutlets **Habitat:** moist to wet sites **Distribution:** native from Newfoundland to Alaska to Texas and around the world **Pick:** a few

Northern Bedstraw

Galium boreale

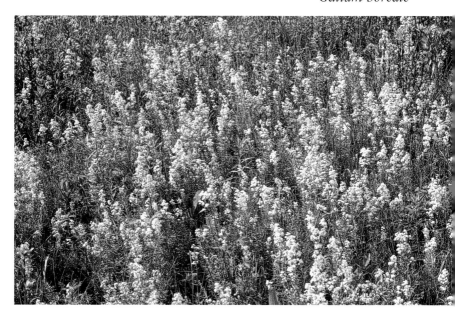

Bedstraw belongs to the same family as coffee, and its tiny nutlets can be roasted as a coffee substitute. The name refers to the historical use of European plants as a fragrant stuffing for mattresses and pillows. Young plants are edible, but more often bedstraw has been used as medicine, often in hot poultices to stop bleeding and reduce swelling. The plant juice has been applied alone or in salves to heal sunburn, rashes, cuts, insect bites, eczema, ringworm and other skin problems. Northern bedstraw tea was traditionally taken to relieve diarrhea, bladder infections and kidney stones, but more recently it has been promoted as a weight-loss aid. Continued use, however, can irritate the mouth and tongue.

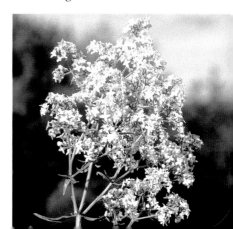

Plant: erect, leafy perennial 20–80 cm tall, with simple or branched, smooth, 4-angled stems
Leaves: in circles (whorls) of 4; narrow, 3-nerved, 1.5–4.5 cm long, stalkless
Flowers: white or creamy, 3.5–7 mm across, with 4 spreading petal lobes; many flowers in showy, branched clusters **Blooms:** June to August **Fruits:** pairs of seed-like nutlets 2 mm long **Habitat:** variable, but not too dry **Distribution:** native from Quebec to Alaska and around the world **Pick:** a few

Curly Dock
Rumex crispus

Tart, lemony dock leaves make a flavourful addition to stews, soups and stir-fries, but they can become distinctly bitter with age. In moderation, the tender young leaves add zing to salads and sandwiches. Like its cousin common rhubarb *(Rheum rhabarbarum)*, curly dock contains oxalic acid, which is toxic in large quantities, but heating and freezing can both destroy this toxin. The seeds were pounded into meal or roasted as a coffee substitute. The fleshy winter roots were collected during spring plowing and cooked as a vegetable. Dried, powdered roots provided a tooth-brushing powder. Some herbalists use dock as a liver stimulant, blood cleanser and mild laxative. • This prolific immigrant is a naturalized weed around the world. Each plant can produce more than 60,000 seeds that are able to survive for up to 80 years.

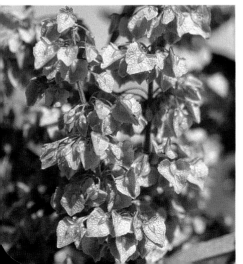

Plant: erect perennial 50–150 cm tall, from taproot **Leaves:** lance-shaped, 10–30 cm long, with finely rippled edges and rounded to notched bases **Flowers:** green or pinkish, with 3 tiny sepals and 3 larger inner flaps (valves); flowers in circles (whorls) in narrow, branched clusters 10–40 cm long **Blooms:** April to July **Fruits:** 3-sided, seed-like achenes enclosed by 3 papery, golden to red-brown, 5 mm long valves, each with a conspicuous wart-like bump
Habitat: moist, often disturbed sites
Distribution: Eurasia; naturalized across Canada and the U.S. **Pick:** freely

Wormseed Wallflower

Erysimum cheiranthoides

The intensely bitter seeds of this plant were once given to children to clear obstructions and flush parasites from the intestines, hence 'wormseed' in the common name. Small doses induced vomiting and diarrhea, but large doses were quite toxic. In North America, various tribes boiled the roots to make washes for healing sores. • All parts of this plant, and especially the seeds, contain toxic mustard oils. Most livestock refuse to eat the pungent, bitter-tasting seed or any feed contaminated with it. • Wormseed wallflower is rarely a problem in cultivated fields, but it can be difficult to control in tame-mustard crops such as canola. It spreads readily, with each plant producing up to 3500 seeds. Most colonies of this common weed are direct descendants of plants that were brought from Europe.

Plant: slightly hairy annual with parallel, flat-lying, T-shaped hairs on erect stems 20–60 cm tall, from taproot **Leaves:** slender to lance-shaped, 2–8 cm long, with flat-lying, 3-pronged hairs **Flowers:** yellow, cross-shaped, 3–5 mm across, on slender, spreading stalks; flowers in dense, rounded, elongating clusters **Blooms:** June to August **Fruits:** slender, erect to ascending, nearly hairless, 4-sided pods 1–3 cm long and 1 mm thick **Habitat:** moist, disturbed sites **Distribution:** introduced (mainly; from Eurasia) and native from Newfoundland to Alaska to Florida and California, and around the world **Pick:** freely

Tumbleweed Mustard

Sisymbrium altissimum

This successful immigrant is native to the western Mediterranean region and to northern Africa. Early settlers and Native peoples sometimes used its small seeds for seasoning, and a few tribes boiled the ground seed to make gruel. Tumbleweed mustard makes a good potherb, but only when the leaves are young and tender, before the plant flowers. Try adding a few young leaves to salads and soups. • Tumbleweed mustard will occasionally infest fields, but it is not usually considered a noxious weed. A single plant can produce up to 2700 seeds. In fall, the dried skeletons of dead plants form airy spheres that break off near the ground and tumble freely in the wind, scattering seeds along the way. • Tumbleweed mustard is also called tall hedge-mustard.

Plant: essentially hairless annual (sometimes biennial) 30–100 cm tall, much branched above **Leaves:** stalked, deeply pinnately cut into slender, often toothed lobes; upper leaves skeleton-like **Flowers:** pale yellow, about 6–14 mm across, cross-shaped, with 4 petals and 4 sepals; flowers borne at branch tips in elongating clusters **Blooms:** June to August **Fruits:** slender, ascending to spreading pods 5–10 cm long, 1–1.5 mm wide, with stalks almost as thick **Habitat:** disturbed ground **Distribution:** Europe; naturalized across North America **Pick:** freely

Wild Mustard

Sinapis arvensis

Wild mustard was brought to North America as a source of cooking greens, mustard seasoning and burning oil. Unfortunately, it is now regarded mainly as a noxious weed. A single plant may produce 3500 seeds, which can survive for up to 60 years, germinating whenever conditions permit. • Many significant crops, including canola and other rapeseed varieties, turnip, cabbage, cauliflower, kale and brown mustard, are species of the genus *Brassica* and are closely related to wild mustard. As a result, wild mustard can be very difficult to identify and control when it invades fields of some of these crops. Not only does wild mustard compete for moisture and nutrients, but its seeds reduce the quality of the oil when mixed with canola. • *S. arvensis* has also been called *Brassica kaber*.

Plant: coarse annual with bristly stems 20–80 cm tall, from slender taproot
Leaves: widest above midleaf, coarsely toothed to lobed, 5–20 cm long
Flowers: yellow, 1.5 cm across, cross-shaped, with 4 petals and 4 sepals; flowers on stout, ascending stalks in elongating clusters **Blooms:** May to July
Fruits: 3–5-nerved, cylindrical pods 1.5–4 cm long, tipped with a 4-sided (sometimes 1-seeded) beak about half as long as the pod **Habitat:** waste places, fields **Distribution:** Eurasia; naturalized across North America **Pick:** freely

Buck-Bean

Menyanthes trifoliata

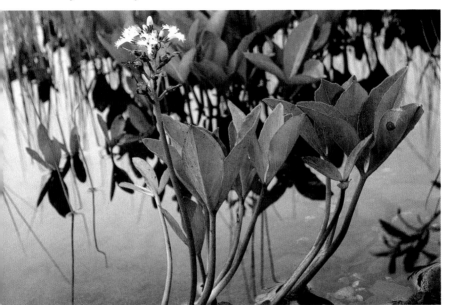

In Europe, powdered buck-bean roots were mixed with flour as a nutritious but bitter bread additive. This practice was especially common in times of famine. More commonly, the bitter leaves were used as a substitute for hops in flavouring beer and were also boiled in honey to make mead. • Buck-bean has been used medicinally for jaundice, indigestion, skin diseases, scurvy, intestinal worms and rheumatism. None of these uses has been proved effective, though the strong-tasting bitters may help stimulate appetite. • Some people recommend buck-bean leaf as a pleasantly bitter addition to summer salads and cream-cheese sandwiches, but only in small quantities. Larger servings cause vomiting and diarrhea.

Plant: fleshy, hairless perennial 10–30 cm tall, from coarse rootstock **Leaves:** basal, long-stalked, divided into 3 leaflets 3–8 cm long, with smooth or wavy edges **Flowers:** white, usually purple-tinged, funnel-shaped, about 2 cm across, with 5 spreading, hairy petals; 10–20 flowers in elongating clusters held just above the water **Blooms:** May to July **Fruits:** thick-walled, egg-shaped capsules 6–9 mm long **Habitat:** standing water **Distribution:** native from Newfoundland to Alaska to the southwestern U.S. and around the world **Pick:** none

Arum-Leaved Arrowhead

Sagittaria cuneata

Although this species is smaller than its better-known cousin wapato *(S. latifolia)*, its fleshy tubers are equally edible. The tubers lie underwater, buried in mud and some distance from the stem, so Native women had to feel around with their toes in icy water to find them. After the miniature 'potatoes' were dislodged, they bobbed to the surface and were skimmed into containers. • Wapato tubers can be 4–5 cm across, but those of arum-leaved arrowhead are much smaller. It takes a lot of energy to gather enough to make a meal, so despite their pleasant flavour (once cooked), these tiny tubers were rarely used. • This common aquatic plant is a valuable source of food for waterfowl and muskrats. People have sometimes raided muskrat push-ups to steal caches of the tasty tubers.

Plant: aquatic perennial; stems 20–50 cm long, from spreading rootstock with fleshy tubers
Leaves: arrowhead-shaped, 1–12 cm long, the 2 lobes shorter than the upper blade; submerged leaves slender, up to 40 cm long **Flowers:** waxy white, about 1 cm across, with 3 petals and 3 sepals; flowers usually in whorls of 3 in elongating clusters with female whorls below male whorls
Blooms: June to August **Fruits:** seed-like achenes, in 1 cm heads **Habitat:** shallow water and muddy shores **Distribution:** native from Labrador to Alaska to Texas **Pick:** none

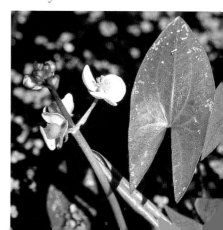

Common Blue-Eyed-Grass

Sisyrinchium montanum

The cheerful blue eyes of this dainty wildflower often seem to float among blades of grass. Without the sun, the flower petals close, and this slender plant disappears among its grassy neighbours. • Common blue-eyed-grass is not a grass at all. Believe it or not, it belongs to the iris family. Try running your fingers along the stems. You'll discover that these stems are distinctly two-sided, not rounded like those of a grass. Also, the leaves attach edgewise to the stem, just like those of a true iris (genus *Iris*). • A few tribes added this plant to medicinal teas for stomachaches, worms and diarrhea, but common blue-eyed-grass has not been widely used. The seeds can take more than two years to germinate, so these delicate blue blooms seldom peek out from flowerbeds.

Plant: slender, clumped perennial 10–50 cm tall, with unbranched, flattened, narrow-winged stems 1–4 mm wide **Leaves:** grass-like, 1–3.5 mm wide **Flowers:** bright violet blue, star-shaped, 6–10 mm across, with 6 abruptly pointed or notched tepals; flowers single or in small clusters from between two 1–6 cm bracts at stem tips **Blooms:** late May to July **Fruits:** round, 3–6 mm capsules on thread-like stalks **Habitat:** moist, open sites **Distribution:** native from Newfoundland to the Yukon, south to North Carolina and Texas **Pick:** a few

Starry False-Solomon's-Seal

Maianthemum stellatum

This graceful native flower is named for its delicate, star-shaped flowers. 'Solomon's-seal' refers to a six-pointed star like the Star of David, and *stellatum* means 'star-like.' • Although the berries can taste sweet, large amounts cause vomiting and diarrhea when eaten raw. The rootstocks were sometimes used for food, but usually they had to be soaked in lye to remove the bitterness, then washed and boiled to remove the lye. Like onions, these fleshy roots were used to flavour other foods. • Medicinally, the roots were chewed raw or used in syrups and teas to relieve coughs. They were also applied as poultices to burns and swellings. The young leaves and shoots are said to be edible, but this lovely plant should be gathered only in an emergency. • This species has also been called *Smilacina stellata*.

Plant: erect perennial 20–60 cm tall, from rootstock **Leaves:** alternate on zigzagged stems, oblong to lance-shaped, 6–15 cm long, usually folded, sometimes clasping **Flowers:** white, 8–10 mm across, with 6 oblong tepals; flowers in elongating, 2–5 cm clusters **Blooms:** May to June **Fruits:** 6–10 mm berries, green with 6 dark stripes at first, blackish red when mature **Habitat:** moist woods, shores and meadows **Distribution:** native from Newfoundland to Alaska, south through the U.S. **Pick:** none

White Death-Camas

Zigadenus elegans

Beware! All parts of this rather innocent-looking wildflower contain toxic chemicals (alkaloids) said to be more potent than strychnine. Sheep (particularly), cattle, horses and chickens have been poisoned by *Zigadenus* species, with losses of up to 2000 animals at a time. Human deaths have usually occurred when the bulbs were mistaken for those of a wild onion (*Allium* spp.) or camas (*Camassia* spp). Just two bulbs can be fatal. Symptoms include salivating, vomiting, diarrhea, lowered body temperature and a slow heartbeat. If you think that someone has eaten these bulbs, encourage vomiting and get the person to a doctor as soon as possible. • *Zigadenus* means 'yoked glands,' referring to the two-lobed gland on each petal. This genus name has also been spelled *Zygadenus*.

Plant: erect perennial 20–60 cm tall, from an onion-like bulb **Leaves:** grass-like, blue-green, mostly basal, up to 1.2 cm wide, with parallel veins **Flowers:** white to greenish white, star-shaped, with 6 oblong, 7–12 mm long tepals each bearing a green, heart-shaped gland near the base; flowers in branched clusters 10–30 cm long **Blooms:** July to August **Fruits:** egg-shaped, 1–1.5 cm long capsules containing angular, 3 mm seeds **Habitat:** moist to wet, open sites **Distribution:** native from Quebec to Alaska, south to Mexico **Pick:** none (abundant, but toxic)

Wood Lily

Lilium philadelphicum

This bright orange wildflower creates splashes of colour along waysides across Canada. It is Saskatchewan's floral emblem.
• Many tribes gathered the bulbs of wood lily for food and medicine. The bulbs are said to have an excellent flavour, either raw or cooked. As well, the abundant, nutritious pollen can be dusted on various dishes. Medicinally, the bulbs were once cooked and then applied to sores, bruises, swellings or wounds. They were also used to make a tea for treating stomach problems, coughs and fevers and for helping women in labour to deliver the afterbirth.
• Wood lilies have disappeared from many populated places. Picking the flowers with their leafy stems or gathering the bulbs kills these beautiful plants. Please leave them for others to enjoy.

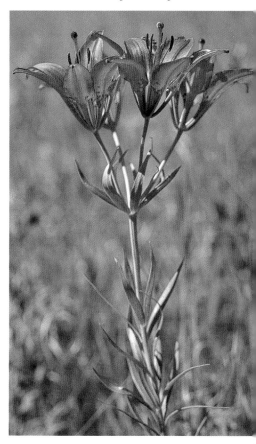

Plant: erect perennial 30–90 cm tall, from bulb 2–3 cm thick **Leaves:** slender, 3–10 cm long, rough-edged, in circles (whorls) of 3–8 upwards on the stem, often alternate below **Flowers:** usually reddish orange (red to yellowish), with 6 purple-spotted tepals, broadly funnel-shaped, 6–10 cm long, held erect; 1–5 flowers per plant **Blooms:** June to August **Fruits:** oblong capsules 4–7 cm long, with packed rows of flat seeds **Habitat:** dry woods, meadows, roadsides **Distribution:** native from Quebec to B.C., south to New Mexico **Pick:** none

Prickly-Pear Cactus

Opuntia polyacantha

Over the years, this spiny resident has been widely used for food. The flat, fleshy pads (stems) were steamed in pits, baked in hot coals or roasted over fires to singe off their spines. Cooked pads could then be peeled or squeezed to extract the soft, cucumber-flavoured flesh, which was mixed with currants and other berries. More recently, it has been added to fruitcakes. • Prickly-pear fruits are sweet and edible, though rather dry. Some Native women made brooms of sagebrush to sweep away large spines and then picked off remaining thorns using deerskin thimbles. The tasty pulp was often used to thicken stews and soups. • Some tribes used small bundles of prickly-pear spines to prick patterns and embed wetted charcoal under the skin, thereby creating tattoos. • This cactus is sometimes called hair-spine prickly-pear.

Plant: succulent, spiny perennial 5–15 cm tall, with fleshy, jointed stems composed of flat segments about 1 cm thick and 5–12 cm long, often clumped or in mats **Leaves:** reduced to short bristles and stiff, barbed spines 1–3.5 cm long; clustered in spirally arranged, white-woolly dots **Flowers:** yellow, bronze with age, 4–7 cm across, with many petals around a large cluster of yellow to orange anthers and a prominent green stigma; flowers stalkless, single at branch tips **Blooms:** June to July **Fruits:** fleshy, slightly spiny, egg-shaped berries 2–5 cm long, pinkish to cream when ripe, containing large, whitish seeds **Habitat:** dry, open sites **Distribution:** native from Saskatchewan to B.C. to Texas **Pick:** a few; caution

Yellow Pond-Lily

Nuphar lutea

Long, slender stalks anchor yellow pond-lily's floating flowers and leaves to deeply buried rootstocks. The stalks contain large air-filled tubes that transport oxygen to the roots and waste gases to the surface. • Native peoples gathered the thick rootstocks in winter and spring, boiled or roasted them for several hours, then peeled them to expose their sweet, gluey contents. Rootstocks were also sliced, dried and ground into meal or flour. The starchy seeds can be hard to remove, so some tribes rotted the fruits to soften them. The heated seeds swell like poor-quality popcorn, making a crunchy snack. • This species includes *N. variegata*.

Plant: aquatic perennial from large rootstock
Leaves: floating (sometimes underwater), round-heart-shaped, 7–35 cm long, on long, narrowly winged stalks **Flowers:** single, cupped, 3.5–6 cm across, with about 6 yellow, petal-like sepals (often reddish inside) and many large (4–7 mm) anthers around a yellowish, 1 cm disc (stigma) with about 10–15 lines radiating from the centre **Blooms:** May to September **Fruits:** egg-shaped, spongy to leathery berries 2–4.5 cm long **Habitat:** quiet waters **Distribution:** native across North America **Pick:** none

Yellow Marsh-Marigold

Caltha palustris

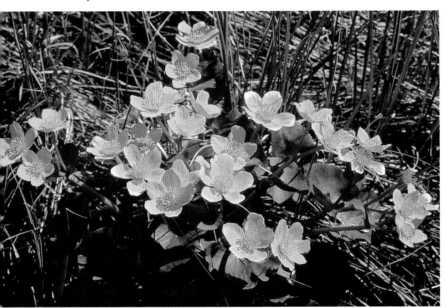

Bright yellow clumps of this shining flower brighten many dark, damp hollows in spring and early summer. Although the buttercup-like blooms appear evenly yellow to human eyes, their petal tips reflect ultraviolet light and their bases absorb it. As a result, insects such as bees, whose eyes detect ultraviolet light, see distinct patterns that direct them to nectaries at the centre of the flower. • Yellow marsh-marigold is sometimes grown as an ornamental in moist, shady gardens. This rather toxic plant has also been used for food and medicine, but it contains strong irritants that can cause blistering, and it is poisonous if eaten raw.

Plant: fleshy perennial 20–60 cm tall, with thick, hollow stems **Leaves:** dark green, heart-shaped to kidney-shaped, 5–17 cm long, shallowly toothed, smaller and more widely notched upwards on the stem **Flowers:** bright, shiny yellow, saucer-shaped, 1.5–4 cm across, with 5–9 petal-like sepals (no petals), 50–120 stamens and a dense cluster of pistils; flowers in branched clusters **Blooms:** April to June **Fruits:** capsules (follicles) 1–1.5 cm long, borne in head-like clusters **Habitat:** wet sites, often in shallow water **Distribution:** native across North America and around the world **Pick:** none; caution

Meadow Buttercup

Ranunculus acris

Some sources suggest meadow buttercup as a lovely addition to the garden, but unsuspecting gardeners will likely find themselves fighting to keep this very prolific European weed at bay. • The specific epithet *acris* describes the acrid sap of this buttercup. The caustic, bitter juice discourages browsers, and it can also blister sensitive skin. • The characteristic shininess of these flowers comes from a specialized film of white cells in the petals that reflects light. Tall stems hold the bright yellow blooms above surrounding plants to attract the attention of pollinating insects. • Meadow buttercup has also been called tall buttercup.

Plant: slender, branched perennial 60–100 cm tall **Leaves:** kidney-shaped, divided into wedge-shaped, deeply lobed parts arranged like fingers on a hand (palmate) **Flowers:** glossy yellow, saucer-shaped, about 2.5 cm across, with 5 broadly ovate petals, 5 greenish, spreading sepals and many stamens and pistils; few to several flowers in loose clusters **Blooms:** May to September **Fruits:** flattened, seed-like achenes 2–3 mm long, with a 0.4–1 mm beak; fruits in round heads **Habitat:** meadows and disturbed habitats **Distribution:** Europe; naturalized across North America **Pick:** freely; caution

Yellow Watercrowfoot

Ranunculus gmelinii

Good names can tell a lot. 'Yellow watercrowfoot' tells us about this plant's flowers, leaves and habitat. The flowers are bright yellow; the leaves have slender lobes that radiate like crow toes; and the plant likes to live in wetlands, usually in shallow water. The scientific name *Ranunculus* comes from the Latin *rana*, 'frog,' another common wetland dweller, referring to the fact that many buttercups prefer marshy areas. Finally, the specific epithet honours Johann Gmelin (1709–55), a German professor of botany and chemistry. Gmelin belonged to a famous family of scientists, and he accompanied Bering in his exploration of Siberia in the 1730s and 1740s. • Yellow watercrowfoot thrives in sloughs across North America. Thoreau described the strong smell of such freshwater marshes as agreeable and invigorating to the imagination, but not everyone agrees with him. • This species has also been called lesser yellow water buttercup.

Plant: creeping or floating perennial with roots from stem joints **Leaves:** deeply cut into 3–5 lobed segments, thick and broad-lobed above water, slender and delicate underwater **Flowers:** yellow, saucer-shaped, about 1.5 cm across, with 5 petals and 5 sepals; 1–4 flowers held above the water on slender stalks **Blooms:** July to August **Fruits:** slender-beaked, seed-like achenes about 1.5 mm long, in head-like clusters 1–4 cm long **Habitat:** muddy shores and calm, shallow water **Distribution:** native from Newfoundland to Alaska to New Mexico and around the world **Pick:** none

Canada Anemone

Anemone canadensis

This common wildflower is easily identified by the circle of coarsely toothed, stalkless leaves high on its flower stems. Anemone flowers have no true petals. Instead, the five showy sepals attract pollinating insects.
• In the western U.S., some tribes attributed mystical powers to Canada anemone and valued its roots as a medicine, applied in washes and poultices. However, anemones contain many of the caustic substances that are common in species of the buttercup family, so handle these plants with care, especially if you have sensitive skin. • Another common name for anemone is windflower. The genus name comes from the Greek *anemos*, 'wind,' because these beautiful flowers were thought to open with the first breezes of spring.

Plant: erect perennial 20–80 cm tall, from spreading rootstock **Leaves:** cut into 3–5 sharply toothed parts; long-stalked at the plant base and stalkless in a circle below the flowers **Flowers:** white, saucer-shaped, 2.5–3.8 cm across, with 5 petal-like sepals (no petals); flowers single or sometimes 2–3 **Blooms:** May to August **Fruits:** seed-like achenes 3–5 mm long, flattened, with flat-lying hairs; achenes in round heads **Habitat:** moist, open sites **Distribution:** native across temperate North America **Pick:** a few; caution

Prairie-Crocus

Pulsatilla patens

This hardy harbinger of spring is Manitoba's floral emblem. Prairie-crocuses often push their way up through snow, spreading a blanket of mauve across the prairie. • Prairie-crocuses may appear delicate, but they are best left alone. Their sap can blister sensitive skin and cause vomiting, tremors and even collapse if any parts are eaten. Most animals avoid eating these caustic plants, so fields of prairie-crocus can be a sign of overgrazing. Even the juice of the purple flowers can irritate, but it was sometimes used to colour Easter eggs—hence the alternative name pasqueflower for the Paschal or Easter season. • *P. patens* has also been called crocus anemone, *P. ludoviciana* and *Anemone patens*.

Plant: tufted, silky-hairy perennial 10–40 cm tall
Leaves: mainly basal, 4–10 cm wide, divided 1–3 times into slender segments, long-stalked; stem leaves smaller, in a ring near midstem, stalkless
Flowers: blue to purple (rarely white), cupped, about 2.5–3.5 cm across, with 5–7 petal-like sepals (no true petals); single **Blooms:** March to June
Fruits: silky-hairy, seed-like achenes tipped with a feathery style 2–4 cm long; achenes in fluffy heads when mature **Habitat:** open, well-drained sites
Distribution: native from western Ontario to Alaska, south through the U.S. **Pick:** a few; caution

Northern Grass-of-Parnassus

Parnassia palustris

Northern grass-of-Parnassus looks innocent, but it's one of nature's tricksters. Its delicate white blossoms have a ring of yellowish green structures called staminodia near their centres. Every staminodium has 7 to 15 slender fingers, each tipped with a shiny knob that mimics a drop of nectar. Small flies flock to this apparent sweet feast. After they land, they are guided to the centre of the flower by prominent pale green or yellow veins on each petal. Having been fooled by the staminodia, they don't bother eating the real stamens, but they do brush past them, picking up loads of pollen. A few days later, the stamens fade, and the stigmas become sticky and ready to receive the pollen carried by insects arriving from other flowers. • This species has also been called marsh grass-of-Parnassus.

Plant: hairless perennial 10–30 cm tall
Leaves: mainly basal, heart-shaped, 0.5–2 cm long, stalked; stem leaf single, heart-shaped, clasping lower stem
Flowers: white, saucer-shaped, about 2 cm across, with 5 sepals, 5 petals, 5 fertile stamens, 5 staminodia (sterile stamens) and an egg-shaped ovary; single
Blooms: July to August **Fruits:** many-seeded capsules 8–12 mm long
Habitat: open or shaded, moist sites
Distribution: native from Newfoundland to Alaska, south through the western U.S. and around the world **Pick:** a few

Field Mouse-Ear-Chickweed

Cerastium arvense

This showy little wildflower can carpet the ground with masses of delicate white flowers. Unfortunately, its efforts aren't always appreciated. Field mouse-ear-chickweed has been designated a weed in Alberta and Manitoba. Although it cannot tolerate plowing and so is not a problem in cultivated fields, it thrives on lawns and in overgrazed pastures. • If you'd like to cultivate this native species, you shouldn't have trouble growing it from seed, which is abundant, or from plant divisions. • Field mouse-ear-chickweed is edible, but its hairiness and small size limit its appeal. Generally it is cooked before it is eaten. • Given its preferred habitat, the name *arvense*, 'of the fields,' is very appropriate.

Plant: grey-green, hairy, sometimes glandular perennial 10–30 cm tall, with tufted or matted stems **Leaves:** paired, 1-nerved, awl-shaped to lance-shaped, 1–4 cm long; main leaf axils usually with small clusters of leaves or short sterile shoots **Flowers:** white, broadly funnel-shaped, 1–2 cm across, with 5 broad, 2-lobed petals and 5 small sepals; few to many flowers on slender, 1–3 cm stalks in open clusters **Blooms:** May to July **Fruits:** curved, cylindrical capsules up to 1.2 cm long, containing golden to reddish brown, bumpy seeds **Habitat:** dry, open sites **Distribution:** native from Newfoundland to Alaska to Georgia and New Mexico and around the world **Pick:** freely

Bladder Campion
Silene vulgaris

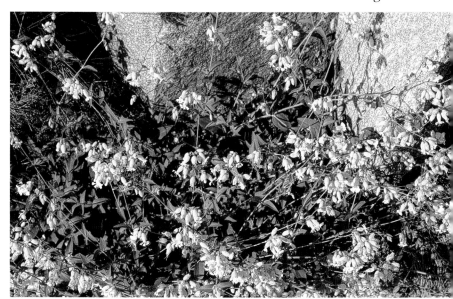

Historically, bladder campion saved lives by providing survival food for the people of Minorca when swarms of locusts destroyed the harvest in 1685. The young leaves, with their sweet, pea-like flavour, were once popular in Europe as a spring potherb. However, the plant becomes very bitter and unpleasant with age as the soap (saponin) content increases. • Bladder campion is a common weed but not a serious problem in planted fields. It produces exquisite urn-shaped capsules that appear to be made of polished wood. These capsules make an interesting addition to dried-flower arrangements. • *S. vulgaris* has also been called *S. cucubalus*.

Plant: bluish green perennial 20–80 cm tall, from deep roots **Leaves:** paired, ovate, 3–10 cm long, often clasping, sometimes fringed **Flowers:** whitish, with 5 white, deeply 2-lobed, 3.5–6 mm wide petal blades sticking out from a papery, grey-green to purple-tinged balloon of fused sepals about 1 cm across; flowers in clusters of 5–30 **Blooms:** April to August **Fruits:** 3-chambered capsules opening by 6 teeth; enclosed in sepal balloons 1–2 cm across **Habitat:** disturbed ground **Distribution:** Europe; naturalized across North America **Pick:** freely

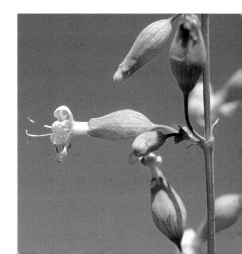

Fringed Yellow-Loosestrife

Lysimachia ciliata

The name 'loosestrife' suggests that this pretty little wildflower should relieve tension, but instead it often creates confusion. Some say *Lysimachia* comes from the Greek *lysis*, or 'loosening,' and *machê*, 'strife,' because it calmed unruly oxen when hung from their yokes. Others believe the name honours the ancient King Lysimachus of Thrace, who discovered its medicinal powers—though it's not at all clear what those powers are. To add to the confusion, the name *Lysimachia* once referred to both a yellow-flowered plant (now called *L. vulgaris*) and a purple-flowered plant (now *Lythrum salicaria*, or purple loosestrife). Plants of both genera have kept the common name loosestrife even though they aren't related. • *L. ciliata* is also known by the name *Steironema ciliata*.

Plant: erect perennial 30–130 cm tall, from creeping underground rootstock **Leaves:** paired, roughly ovate, 4–14 cm long, with prominently fringed stalks **Flowers:** yellow, 1.5–2.5 cm across, saucer-shaped, with 5 abruptly slender-pointed petals, 5 sepals, 5 fertile stamens, 5 sterile stamens and 1 style; flowers borne on slender, 1.5–6.5 cm stalks from leaf axils **Blooms:** June to August **Fruits:** small, rounded capsules **Habitat:** moist to wet sites **Distribution:** native from Quebec to B.C., Alaska, southern U.S. **Pick:** a few

Saline Shootingstar

Dodecatheon pulchellum

One glance at this wildflower explains the name. A pointed nose of anthers shoots downward from five pinkish purple, upswept petals that resemble streaming tails on a shooting star. This distinctive floral structure has inspired many fanciful monikers, including 'rain's-navel' (Haida), 'beautiful-maiden' (Thompson) and 'mad-violet' (Italian). • Saline shootingstar is highly variable, with plants ranging from hairless to densely glandular-hairy. Also, the yellow band at the base of the anthers can be orange or even reddish purple. • Some tribes considered shootingstars a sure charm for prosperity and luck in love. Women used the flowers to try to control men. Not only did shootingstars bring wealth, they created in others a strong urge to shower the charmer with gifts. • This species has also been called dark-throated shootingstar and *D. pauciflorum*.

Plant: perennial 5–30 cm (rarely 50 cm) tall, with leafless stems from short rootstock **Leaves:** ovate to spoon-shaped, 3–20 cm long, smooth- or wavy-edged **Flowers:** magenta to lavender, about 1.5–2.5 cm across, with 5 showy petals swept up from a yellow collar around a purplish nose of fused, 3–8 mm long anthers on 0.5–3.5 mm filaments; about 3–12 flowers nodding in loose clusters **Blooms:** May to August **Fruits:** capsules 5–15 mm long, opening by 5 teeth **Habitat:** moist, open sites **Distribution:** native from Saskatchewan to Alaska to Arizona **Pick:** none

Three-Flowered Avens

Geum triflorum

Settlers affectionately called three-flowered avens colourful names such as 'old man's whiskers' and 'prairie smoke.' The fluffy fruiting heads looked like the wispy beard of an old man, and when plants grew in profusion they spread a smoke-like haze across the prairie. • A pleasant tea, made from the fragrant pink roots, was widely used as a beverage and also as a medicine for treating colds, flu and fevers. Avens plants are astringent and cause soft tissues to pucker, so the root tea can help to reduce bleeding and inflammation. The tea was used to treat diarrhea and dysentery and to soothe sore eyes, mouths and throats. In the sweathouse, the roots were boiled to make a purifying wash for relieving aches and pains.

Plant: reddish, soft-hairy perennial 10–30 cm tall, from stout rootstock **Leaves:** mainly basal, 5–20 cm long, pinnately divided into many toothed or lobed leaflets **Flowers:** purplish to dusty pink, urn-shaped, about 2 cm across, nodding; in loose clusters of 3 (sometimes 1–9) **Blooms:** May to July **Fruits:** seed-like achenes 3 mm long, tipped with a feathery, 2–4 cm bristle (the elongated style); fruits form erect, fluffy heads **Habitat:** open, well-drained sites **Distribution:** native from Ontario to B.C., south through the western U.S. **Pick:** a few

Yellow Avens

Geum aleppicum

This widespread plant has been used for medicine all around the world. North American Native peoples boiled the roots to make teas for coughs, sore mouths and throats, chest congestion, diarrhea and fever. In China, it was used to treat bug bites, convulsions, fever, nervous irritability, skin diseases and painful sores and wounds.
• Large clumps of yellow avens make a showy addition to wildflower gardens, but beware of the burs. Every blossom produces a bristling head of tiny, clinging fruits that latch onto passersby. These very persistent hangers-on gave rise to the Cree name 'jealousy plant,' and because of this clinging quality, men used yellow avens as a love charm. Women thus afflicted mixed it into their antidotes.

Plant: erect, coarse-hairy perennial 40–100 cm tall, from short rootstock
Leaves: mainly basal, pinnately divided into 5–7 main leaflets interspersed with smaller leaflets; tip leaflet largest, tapered to a wedge-shaped base
Flowers: bright yellow, saucer-shaped, 1–2.5 cm across, with 5 petals and 5 sepals; flowers in open, flat-topped clusters **Blooms:** June to July
Fruits: hairy, seed-like achenes 3–4 mm long, tipped with a hooked 4–6 mm bristle; fruits in bur-like heads 1–1.5 cm wide **Habitat:** moist sites
Distribution: native from Quebec to Alaska to Georgia and New Mexico, and around the world **Pick:** a few

Virginia Strawberry
Fragaria virginiana

Although its delicate blooms are easily overlooked, Virginia strawberry is one of our commonest wildflowers. Most people know this little plant for its fruits rather than its flowers. Wild strawberries may be small, but each one packs all the flavour of a larger domestic strawberry. • A tea made from strawberry leaves provides a refreshing drink that is rich in vitamin C and minerals. For centuries, it has been used as a safe (but not necessarily effective) remedy for everything from insanity to tuberculosis. This tea is still widely used to treat diarrhea and skin problems. If you decide to try strawberry-leaf tea, use only fresh or completely dried leaves, because the wilted leaves contain toxins. • Virginia strawberry has also been called smooth wild strawberry.

Plant: low perennial, often with slender runners
Leaves: basal, long-stalked, with 3 coarsely toothed leaflets each tipped with a relatively small tooth **Flowers:** white, 5-petalled, saucer-shaped, 1.5–2 cm across; in small clusters **Blooms:** April to June **Fruits:** strawberries, with seed-like achenes in pits on the surface of a round, red, fleshy, 1–1.5 cm sphere **Habitat:** dry to moist, sunny to shaded, often disturbed sites **Distribution:** native across North America **Pick:** a few (flowers or fruits)

Yellow Mountain-Avens

Dryas drummondii

In flower, the shy mountain-avens is easily overlooked, but when the fluffy seed heads rise above their leafy mats, the plant is hard to miss. This hardy species is wonderfully adapted to the rigours of mountain and arctic life. Waxy, leathery leaves with woolly undersides conserve valuable moisture. The ground-hugging plants seek shelter from cold, drying winds and windblown grit and ice crystals, so that flowers stay in the layer of calmer, warmer air near the ground. Here, pollinating insects visit more easily and fruits develop more rapidly. Dense evergreen mats trap debris, accumulating soil. Tough roots stretch deep for moisture and nutrients and produce extra nitrogen from bacteria in special nodules—a definite advantage when you're growing on gravel. • *Dryas* was named for the Dryades, daughters of Zeus and nymphs of the oak, because the leaves of these little plants were likened to tiny oak leaves.

Plant: low, mat-forming perennial
Leaves: thick, tapered to a wedge-shaped base, 1–3 cm long, round-toothed
Flowers: yellow, funnel- to bell-shaped, 1–2 cm long, with 8–10 petals and 8–10 blackish, glandular-hairy sepals; flowers single, nodding **Blooms:** June to August
Fruits: seed-like achenes 2–3 mm long, tipped with a feathery, 3–4 cm bristle (style); fruits in fluffy heads when mature
Habitat: open, well-drained sites
Distribution: native from Newfoundland to Alaska (absent from central Canada) to Idaho
Pick: a few

Common Silverweed

Argentina anserina

This charming little 'rose' often forms carpets of silver and green leaves dotted with sunny yellow flowers. Although it is easily overlooked, common silverweed is a circumpolar plant with an interesting history. In western Scotland, its starchy roots are said to have saved entire villages from starvation during famines. Raw, boiled or roasted, the spring roots have been likened to parsnips, chestnuts and sweet potatoes. Medicinally, common silverweed was used mainly as an astringent in gargles, washes and teas for reducing inflammation and stopping bleeding of the digestive tract, kidneys and skin. • *A. anserina* has also been called *Potentilla anserina*.

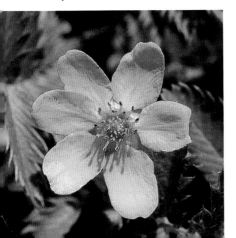

Plant: low perennial with slender, creeping runners **Leaves:** basal, up to 30 cm long, silvery-hairy and woolly underneath, pinnately divided into many sharply toothed leaflets with small and large leaflets interspersed **Flowers:** yellow, 1.5–2.5 cm across, with 5 petals above 5 sepals and 5 smaller, alternating bractlets; flowers single **Blooms:** May to September **Fruits:** thick, furrowed, seed-like achenes 2.5 mm long, in dense heads **Habitat:** well-drained to wet, open sites **Distribution:** native across North America and around the world **Pick:** a few

Shrubby Cinquefoil

Dasiphora fruticosa

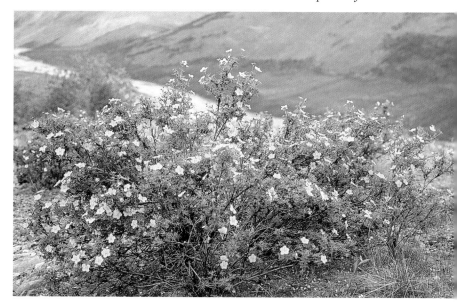

This hardy shrub with its abundant yellow flowers is common in parks and gardens, so travellers may be surprised to see it in the wild. Such plants have not escaped cultivation. Rather, shrubby cinquefoil is a widespread native shrub that has become popular with gardeners. • The stems and leaves were once steeped to make a tea for relieving fevers, coughs and diarrhea. Little evidence supports these medicinal uses, but the tea is considered pleasant and nontoxic. • Some tribes believed that shrubby cinquefoil contained a deadly heart poison, which was applied to arrow tips and porcupine quills for wounding the enemy. • *D. fruticosa* has also been called *Potentilla fruticosa* and *Pentaphylloides floribunda*.

Plant: deciduous shrub 10–100 cm tall, with shredding, reddish brown bark **Leaves:** greyish green, pinnately divided into 3–7 (usually 5) narrowly oblong leaflets 1–2 cm long **Flowers:** saucer-shaped, 1.5–3 cm across, with 5 broad petals, 5 sepals and 5 smaller alternating bractlets; flowers clustered at branch tips **Blooms:** June to September **Fruits:** pale brown, seed-like achenes **Habitat:** open, wet to well-drained sites **Distribution:** native from Newfoundland to Alaska to New Mexico and around the world **Pick:** a few

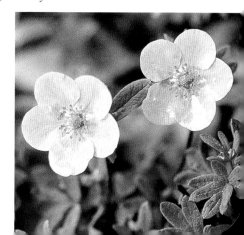

Plains Cinquefoil
Potentilla bipinnatifida

The name *Potentilla*, from *potens*, 'potent,' refers to cinquefoils' supposed medicinal powers, especially their ability to stop bleeding and diarrhea in both human and beast. But despite their name, *Potentilla* species are not widely used for medicine. Like most members of the rose family, these plants contain tannins, which constrict soft tissues, but other astringent medicines are generally preferred. Cinquefoil tea has sometimes been used to treat fevers, diarrhea and mouth or throat infections. Young leaves produce a pleasant, golden, calcium-rich tea, but the plants soon become quite bitter. • Tannin-rich cinquefoils have also been used to tan hides and to give leather a beautiful reddish colour. With a chrome mordant, the crushed roots dye wool red-brown, and with iron the wool takes on a purplish red hue. The flowers make a bright yellow dye.

Plant: clumped, usually hairy, erect perennial 20–50 cm tall, from stout root crown **Leaves:** grey-green above, white-woolly underneath, about 10–25 cm long, long-stalked, pinnately divided into 3–7 leaflets (sometimes appearing palmate); leaflets 3–6 cm long, deeply cut into 1.5–3 mm wide lobes **Flowers:** yellow, 6–10 mm across, with 5 small petals, 5 conspicuous sepals (longer than petals) and 5 smaller alternating bractlets; flowers in branched clusters **Blooms:** July to August **Fruits:** seed-like achenes 1 mm long **Habitat:** dry, open sites **Distribution:** native from Newfoundland to Alaska to New Hampshire and Arizona **Pick:** a few

Graceful Cinquefoil
Potentilla gracilis

The bright yellow blooms of graceful cinquefoil make a lovely addition to wildflower gardens. Wild plants often produce large quantities of fertile seeds that can be sown without special treatment. • An abundance of nectar and pollen attracts many insects to these showy flowers. Once a flower has been pollinated, its bracts and sepals fold upwards in a tight bundle with the developing seeds protected inside. When the seeds ripen, the outer layers loosen slightly, and as the stems sway in the breeze they scatter the seeds. • Mashed leaves and roots of this plant were sometimes mixed with fir resin to make pain-relieving salves for wounds. • Graceful cinquefoil is a highly variable species. Different varieties have leaves that range from green to densely white-woolly (especially on the undersides), and from shallowly round-toothed to deeply sharp-toothed.

Plant: erect perennial 30–70 cm tall, from scaly crown **Leaves:** long-stalked, palmately divided into 5–9 leaflets; leaflets lance-shaped, widest above midleaf, coarsely toothed or lobed **Flowers:** yellow, saucer-shaped, 1.5–2 cm across, with 5 petals above 5 sepals and 5 alternating bractlets; numerous flowers in branched, flat-topped clusters **Blooms:** June to July **Fruits:** egg-shaped, seed-like achenes, tipped with a slender style **Habitat:** dry, open sites **Distribution:** native from Quebec to Alaska to Arizona **Pick:** a few

Prickly Rose

Rosa acicularis

On warm days in summer, these beautiful blossoms—Alberta's floral emblem—emit a delicate fragrance. But beware! The name *acicularis*, 'needle-like,' refers to the abundant protective prickles. • Fragrant rose petals have long been used in potpourris, scented oils and perfumes. In the kitchen, rose flowers make a fine, delicately flavoured tea or can be added to salads, fruit punches and sandwiches. Outdoors, the petals provide a melt-in-your-mouth nibble likened to perfumed bubblegum. • For centuries, the sweet, red flesh of rose hips has been used for food and as a source of vitamin C. However, the hairy achenes inside can cause 'itchy bottom' and should not be eaten. Rose hips make excellent jelly, syrup, tea and wine and are a valuable winter emergency food.

Plant: prickly deciduous shrub 20–120 cm tall **Leaves:** sharply toothed, pinnately divided into 5–7 oblong leaflets 3–4 cm long **Flowers:** pink, saucer-shaped, 5–7 cm across, with 5 petals, 5 slender sepals and numerous stamens; flowers in small, loose clusters on short branches **Blooms:** June to August **Fruits:** scarlet hips, berry-like, 1.5–3 cm long, containing hairy, seed-like achenes **Habitat:** dry to moist sites **Distribution:** native from Quebec to Alaska to the central U.S.; also Eurasia **Pick:** a few; caution

Rusty Labrador-Tea

Ledum groenlandicum

This aromatic plant was once used as insect and rodent repellent, but today it is known for its use in making a sweet, fragrant tea. Many aboriginal names are variations upon the English word 'tea,' suggesting this use was introduced by Europeans. • In large quantities, Labrador-tea leaves can cause headaches, delirium, palpitations and paralysis, and boiling releases even more toxins. The tea, though, seems to have variable effects. Some people become drowsy, others feel no change and still others report a caffeine-like effect. This beverage should be introduced cautiously, never boiled and always used in moderation. • Rust-coloured hairs on the leaf undersides distinguish Labrador-tea from its poisonous relatives: mountain laurel *(Kalmia)* and bog rosemary *(Andromeda)* have hairless, whitish lower leaf surfaces. • *L. groenlandicum* has also been called *L. palustre* var. *latifolium*.

Plant: evergreen shrub 30–80 cm tall, in colonies from spreading rootstock
Leaves: leathery, deep green, rusty-hairy underneath, oblong, 1–5 cm long, with down-rolled edges **Flowers:** white, about 1 cm across, on long, white-hairy stalks; flowers in rounded clusters at branch tips
Blooms: June to July **Fruits:** nodding, 5-parted capsules 5–7 mm long
Habitat: bogs to moderately dry sites
Distribution: native from Newfoundland to Alaska to the northern U.S.; Greenland
Pick: a few

Northern Crane's-Bill

Geranium bicknellii

The delicate flowers of northern crane's-bill produce narrow, pointed capsules that look like slender beaks, hence the common name. When the capsules mature, they split open from bottom to top, releasing seeds in all directions. Five curled strips remain at the tip, like upcurved arms on a fairy candelabra. • Astringent crane's-bill roots have been used in gargles for mouth and throat sores, in teas for diarrhea and internal bleeding, and in washes for sores and wounds. • Red-stem stork's-bill *(Erodium cicutarium)*, a noxious European weed, can be confused with northern crane's-bill. Stork's-bill is distinguished by its pinnately divided (not palmate) leaves and by its spirally coiled (not simply upcurved) capsule segments.

Plant: erect to sprawling annual or biennial 10–60 cm tall, freely branched, from slender taproot
Leaves: roughly 5-sided, 2–7 cm across, deeply cut into 5 toothed, wedge-shaped segments arranged like fingers on a hand (palmate) **Flowers:** pink to rose purple, about 1 cm across, with 5 notched petals and 5 sepals; flowers paired, on slender, glandular-hairy stalks **Blooms:** May to August **Fruits:** cylindrical capsules about 2 cm long, tapered to a beak 4–6 mm long **Habitat:** open, often disturbed sites **Distribution:** native from Newfoundland to Alaska to Tennessee and California **Pick:** a few

Wild Blue Flax

Linum lewisii

Through the years, wild flax has been widely used for both food and fibre. As food, flax seeds were usually roasted and ground. Roasting breaks down the small amounts of hydrocyanic acid in raw seeds, making them safe to eat in quantity, and grinding increases the available fibre and releases valuable oils. The strong stem fibres were used to make thread, cord, fishing nets and even snowshoe webbing. • Enjoy this lovely wildflower where it grows, for the delicate blooms wilt within minutes of picking. On every stalk, a single flower opens in the morning and closes by late afternoon. The following morning, the next bloom opens, and the developing seed capsule of the previous flower begins to enlarge. • This species has also been called prairie flax, Lewis wild flax and *L. perenne.*

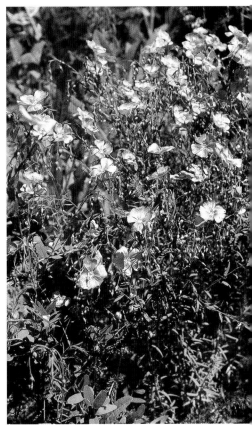

Plant: grey-green, hairless perennial 20–70 cm tall, with erect, slender stems from branched, woody rootstock
Leaves: many, slender, mostly 1-nerved, 1–2.5 cm long **Flowers:** pale blue to sky blue (rarely white), broadly funnel-shaped, about 2–3.5 cm across, with 5 fragile petals and 5 hairless sepals; flowers borne on arched branches, in open clusters **Blooms:** May to August
Fruits: round capsules 5–9 mm across, on curved stalks **Habitat:** dry, open sites
Distribution: native from Ontario to Alaska, south through the U.S. **Pick:** a few

Scarlet Globe-Mallow
Sphaeralcea coccinea

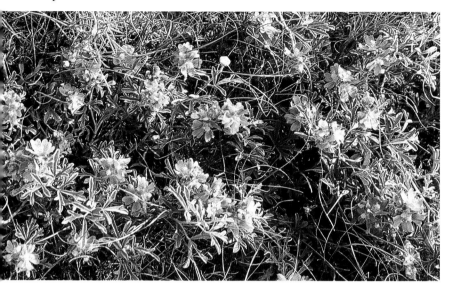

Globe-mallow plants contain lots of mucilage, so they are very slimy inside. The leaves were chewed or crushed to make cooling poultices, used for soothing sores, wounds, inflamed skin and blistered feet. The flowers and leaves were chewed or made into tea for relieving upset stomachs and sore throats. This pleasant drink was also used as a tonic to improve appetite and sweeten bitter medicines. In some tribes, spiritual leaders chewed scarlet globe-mallow plants into paste that they rubbed onto their skin for protection from scalding. With this shield they were said to amaze spectators by reaching into boiling kettles for chunks of hot meat. • *S. coccinea* has also been called *Malvastrum coccineum*.

Plant: low perennial 10–20 cm tall, with dense, star-shaped hairs **Leaves:** yellowish green, grey-hairy underneath, deeply cut into 3–5 wedge-shaped, 2–5 cm long segments arranged like fingers on a hand (palmate) **Flowers:** orange to brick red, 1–2 cm across, with 5 broad, shallowly notched petals and 5 small sepals; flowers in compact clusters at stem tips **Blooms:** May to August **Fruits:** hairy discs composed of many 1-seeded segments, resembling wedges in a wheel of cheese **Habitat:** dry, open sites **Distribution:** native from Manitoba to Alberta, south through the U.S. **Pick:** a few

Common Fireweed

Chamerion angustifolium

Common fireweed will usually grow in small colonies along roads, but after fires it can blanket charred landscapes with a sea of rose purple flowers. The sweet blooms provide a tasty nibble, a pretty salad garnish and abundant nectar for golden fireweed honey. The tender young plants (under 20 cm in height) have been likened to asparagus and eaten in the same way. Around the world, people drink fireweed tea and cook the leaves as a potherb. Like any new food, it should be introduced gradually; the uninitiated may find fireweed quite laxative.
• Older fireweed stems have been split lengthwise to scrape out the soft, edible centre (pith) and to prepare the tough stem fibres for making twine and fishnets.
• *C. angustifolium* is also known as *Epilobium angustifolium*.

Plant: erect perennial 50–300 cm tall, from spreading rootstock
Leaves: many, alternate, lance-shaped
Flowers: purplish pink (rarely white), about 2.5 cm across, with 4 slender-based petals, 4 sepals, 8 stamens and a cross-shaped stigma; flowers in spike-like clusters **Blooms:** June to September
Fruits: slender 3–8 cm pods, splitting lengthwise to release tiny seeds with silky parachutes **Habitat:** highly variable, often disturbed **Distribution:** native across North America and around the world **Pick:** a few

Common Evening-Primrose
Oenothera biennis

Each evening a single delicate flower of common evening-primrose unfurls, releasing its perfume to attract night-flying moths. By noon the following day, the bloom has faded, but if it was pollinated by a moth, its seeds have already started to develop. • Each plant can produce about 6000 oil-rich seeds. North American farmers harvest hundreds of tonnes of evening-primrose seeds each year. The oil from these seeds contains fatty acids that the human body needs in order to produce important hormones. Studies have shown that evening-primrose oil can help treat eczema, asthma, migraine headaches, heart disease, high cholesterol, inflammation, PMS, breast problems, multiple sclerosis, diabetes, rheumatoid arthritis and even alcoholism.

Plant: erect biennial (usually), 50–150 cm tall **Leaves:** lance-shaped to oblong, mostly 10–20 cm long, smooth- or wavy-edged **Flowers:** yellow, 2.5–5 cm across, with a long tube (containing the ovary) below 4 petals, 4 sepals, 8 stamens and a protruding style tipped with a cross-shaped stigma; flowers in stiff, leafy-bracted spikes **Blooms:** July to September **Fruits:** erect, persistent, oblong capsules 1.5–4 cm long
Habitat: disturbed ground
Distribution: native across southern Canada and most of the U.S.
Pick: a few

Great Mullein
Verbascum thapsus

Great mullein was introduced to North America in the 1700s as a medicinal herb, and within 100 years, it had spread across the continent. Each plant produces some 150,000 tiny seeds (four fit on the head of a pin). • The large, fuzzy leaves have been used as diapers and toilet paper, but their tiny hairs can irritate sensitive skin. Women who didn't have makeup sometimes reddened their cheeks by rubbing with mullein leaves, leading to the alternative common name Quaker rouge. Tall, thick stalks of mullein, dipped in melted fat, were burned as torches, which were believed both to repel witches and to be used by them. By a similar contradiction, it was believed that wearing mullein leaves ensured conception, but placing a leaf in one's shoe protected against it.

Plant: stout, grey-woolly biennial 1–2 m tall **Leaves:** thick, felted, up to 30 cm long, in a basal rosette (1st year) and alternate (2nd year), smaller upwards and often with edges extending down stem **Flowers:** yellow, 1–2.5 cm across, with 5 spreading petal lobes, 5 fuzzy sepals, 5 stamens and 1 style; flowers in dense spikes 20–50 cm long **Blooms:** June to September **Fruits:** 2-parted capsules **Habitat:** disturbed sites **Distribution:** Europe; naturalized from Newfoundland to B.C., Alaska and Texas **Pick:** freely; caution

Spreading Dogbane
Apocynum androsaemifolium

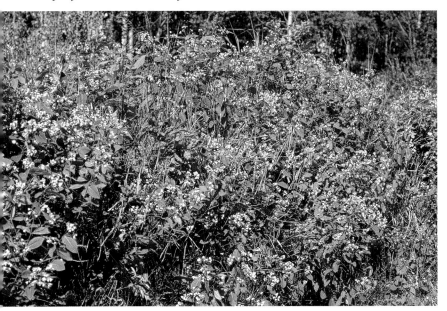

Danger lurks in these delicate bells. Each flower conceals five nectaries inside five V-shaped openings edged with tiny teeth. Insects, drawn to the fragrant nectar, often catch their feet in these openings and cannot escape. Fortunately, bees and butterflies are strong enough to free themselves and carry pollen to other flowers. • Women of some tribes rolled dogbane stem fibres on their legs to make thread. It was used for sewing and for making twine, nets, fabric and bowstrings. The poisonous, acrid sap was said to stimulate hair growth by irritating the follicles, but people with sensitive skin are more likely to develop blisters than hair.

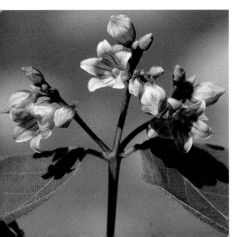

Plant: erect, blue-green perennial 20–100 cm tall, usually bushy, with milky sap
Leaves: paired, 3–10 cm long, often drooping
Flowers: pinkish, bell-shaped, 6–10 mm across, with 5 spreading lobes; flowers nodding on slender stalks in branched clusters
Blooms: June to August **Fruits:** hanging, paired, slender follicles 5–15 cm long, splitting to release seeds with silky white parachutes **Habitat:** sunny, well-drained sites
Distribution: native from Newfoundland to Alaska to southern U.S. **Pick:** freely; caution

Fringed Gromwell

Lithospermum incisum

Many tribes boiled or roasted the large taproots of fringed gromwell for food, but this use is not recommended. Gromwells contain alkaloids that can cause internal bleeding, and they produce estrogen-like compounds that interfere with hormonal balance. • Like violets (pp. 45, 46), gromwells produce another set of flowers later in summer. These blooms never open. Instead, they fertilize themselves and generally produce most of the plant's seed. • The name *Lithospermum*, from the Greek *lithos*, 'stone,' and *sperma*, 'seed,' refers to the hard, stone-like nutlets. • Fringed gromwell has also been called narrow-leaved puccoon. 'Puccoon' comes from an Algonkian word meaning 'plants used for dyeing.' The juicy, red roots were dipped in hot deer fat, and the grease was rubbed on faces and tanned hides as a purplish paint.

Plant: hairy perennial 10–50 cm tall, from deep taproot **Leaves:** slender, 1–5 cm long, with stiff, flat-lying hairs **Flowers:** bright yellow, trumpet-shaped, 1–2 cm across, with a 2 cm tube ending in 5 spreading, fringed petal lobes; flowers in clusters at stem tips **Blooms:** May to June **Fruits:** shiny, ivory white nutlets 3 mm long, sparsely dotted with tiny pits **Habitat:** dry, open sites **Distribution:** native from Ontario to B.C., south through the U.S. **Pick:** a few

Common Viper's-Bugloss

Echium vulgare

Common viper's-bugloss was introduced to North America as a garden flower in the 1600s; by the mid-1800s, agriculturalists were condemning it as a vile foreign weed. Although it is said to be edible, it would make a rather bristly dish. In fact, some people get rashes by simply touching this hairy plant. The beautiful flowers, on the other hand, make a pretty garnish when floated in punch or tossed in salads. • At one time, common viper's-bugloss was said to have the power to drive away sadness, especially when combined with wine. It was also believed to counteract viper venom, and therefore to cure all snake bites. Unfortunately, it was most effective when administered before the bite, which required a certain amount of foresight.

Plant: rough-hairy biennial 30–80 cm tall, from taproot **Leaves:** oblong to lance-shaped, 6–25 cm long, smaller upwards **Flowers:** bright blue to purple (buds pink), asymmetrically funnel-shaped, 1.2–2 cm across, with 4 reddish stamens and a slender style projecting from the mouth; many flowers in elongating clusters with uncoiling, 1-sided branches **Blooms:** June to August **Fruits:** 4 small, rough nutlets **Habitat:** disturbed sites **Distribution:** Europe and north Africa; naturalized from Newfoundland to B.C., Alaska and Texas **Pick:** freely; caution

Tall Bluebells
Mertensia paniculata

If you take a close look at these flower clusters, you'll see that not all of the bells are blue. Flowers that have been pollinated and young buds look pinkish, whereas mature blooms, ready for pollination, turn blue. Many insects are attracted to blue but can't see red or pink, so they fly to the receptive blue flowers and don't bother with the pink ones. The hanging, bell-shaped corolla shelters the reproductive parts and discourages visits from many insects too small to pollinate the flower but still capable of stealing valuable nectar and pollen. • This hardy, shade-tolerant plant, with its attractive blue bells, makes a lovely addition to wildflower gardens. The large basal leaves were sometimes dried, crushed and smoked, often mixed with tobacco. • Tall bluebells has also been called tall lungwort.

Plant: rough-hairy perennial 30–100 cm tall **Leaves:** coarse, stiff-hairy, 5–14 cm long, heart-shaped at the stem base, progressively narrower and shorter-stalked upwards **Flowers:** blue (fading to pink or white), 1–1.5 cm long, funnel-shaped; corolla with a tubular base and flaring, 5-lobed mouth; calyx hairy, with 5 slender lobes; flowers nodding, in elongating clusters **Blooms:** June to August **Fruits:** 4 wrinkled nutlets **Habitat:** moist, often wooded sites **Distribution:** native across Canada, south to the northern U.S. **Pick:** a few

Harebell

Campanula rotundifolia

This delicate, nodding wild-flower is the famous bluebell of Scotland. Although harebell is a hardy, resilient plant, it is also the essence of fragility, with its graceful blue bells bobbing on hair-like stems. Small insects find it difficult to crawl inside these flowers to steal pollen and nectar, but bees and other flying pollinators have easy access. • The nodding bells trap warm air and protect styles and stamens from rain. Mature capsules sway back and forth on slender elastic stalks, scattering the seeds from holes in their sides like swinging salt shakers. • The epithet for this species, *rotundifolia*, refers to the rounded leaves at the bottom of the plant. These basal leaves have usually withered away by the time the flowers open, and only the slender stem leaves remain.

Plant: slender perennial 10–80 cm tall
Leaves: mainly on stem, slender, stalk-less, 1.5–8 cm long; rounded, stalked basal leaves also present but soon fade
Flowers: blue, bell-shaped, 5-lobed, 1.5–2.5 cm long; 1 to many nodding on thread-like stalks in loose, elongating clusters **Blooms:** June to September
Fruits: nodding capsules, opening by pores on the sides near the base
Habitat: well-drained, often rocky sites
Distribution: native across North America south to Mexico, and around the world **Pick:** a few

Field Bindweed

Convolvulus arvensis

Field bindweed is a twining plant with charming, morning-glory-like flowers. Unfortunately, it can soon become a troublesome weed, clambering over other plants in a smothering blanket. The genus name comes from the Latin *convolvere*, 'to entwine.' Field bindweed's tendrils wind tightly around any nearby slender support and can complete a 360° twist every 100 minutes. • Although each plant is capable of producing more than 500 long-lived seeds, field bindweed seldom fruits. Instead, plants usually reproduce by vegetative means. Rootstocks can stretch out 4 m, sending up new shoots along the way. When broken, even small pieces of these deep, brittle runners can become new plants. Newly established bindweed plants also release toxins into the soil to poison other species and reduce competition for water, nutrients and sunlight.

Plant: slender, trailing or climbing perennial, with 30–100 cm stems from deep, spreading rootstock **Leaves:** triangular to arrowhead-shaped, 2–5 cm long **Flowers:** white to pink, broadly funnel-shaped, 1.5–2.5 cm across, twisted in bud; flowers single or paired on long stalks from leaf axils **Blooms:** May to September **Fruits:** small, cone-shaped capsules, usually hanging **Habitat:** disturbed ground **Distribution:** Europe; naturalized across southern Canada and throughout the U.S. **Pick:** freely

Page numbers indicate where terms are illustrated.

achene: a small, dry fruit that does not split open when mature, often seed-like in appearance, distinguished from a nutlet by its relatively thin wall (pp. 12, 150)

alternate: situated singly at each joint or node (e.g., as leaves on a stem) or regularly between other organs (e.g., as stamens alternate with petals) (p. 148)

annual: a plant that completes its life cycle in 1 growing season

anther: the pollen-bearing part of a stamen (pp. 11, 12)

ascending: growing upwards on an angle

axil: the angle between a side organ (e.g., a leaf) and the part to which it is attached (e.g., a stem) (p. 148)

basal: located at the base or arising from it, e.g., leaves at the base of a stem (p. 148)

beak: a prolonged, more or less slender tip on a thicker organ such as a fruit (p. 150)

berry: a fleshy fruit, usually with several to many seeds

biennial: living for 2 years, usually producing flowers and seed in the 2nd year

bilaterally symmetrical: divisible into 2 equal parts along 1 line only (p. 18); compare 'radially symmetrical'

blade: the broad, flat part of a leaf or petal (p. 148)

bract: a specialized leaf with a flower (or sometimes a flower cluster) arising from its axil (pp. 12, 150)

bulb: a fleshy underground organ with overlapping, swollen scales, e.g., an onion

calyx: the sepals of a flower, collectively (p. 11)

LEAF PARTS AND ARRANGEMENTS

capsule: a dry fruit that splits open when mature, often with more than 1 seed (p. 150)

chambered: with inner cavities

circumpolar: found in northern areas around the world

clambering: sprawling and trailing over the ground

clasping: embracing or surrounding, usually in reference to a leaf base around a stem (p. 148)

compound: divided into smaller parts (p. 149)

corolla: the petals of a flower, collectively (p. 11)

creeping: growing along (or beneath) the surface of the ground and producing roots and sometimes shoots at intervals (usually at joints)

crown: the part of a plant where the stems and roots meet

cultivar: a cultivated variety, i.e., a plant or animal originating in cultivation

drupe: a fleshy, pulpy, 1-seeded fruit with a stony covering on the seed (p. 150), e.g., a cherry pit

elongating cluster: a flower cluster that lengthens as it develops, with flowers and fruits forming at the base first and then upwards to the tip (p. 150); a raceme

family: a group of related plants or animals forming a category of biological classification above genus, e.g., the aster family (Asteraceae); see p. 154 for a list of all families in this book

fibrous roots: slender, fibre-like roots, usually numerous and clumped

fleshy: plump, firm and pulpy; succulent

floret: a small flower, usually 1 of several in a cluster (pp. 12, 18)

flowerhead: a dense cluster of tiny flowers (florets), often appearing as a single flower (pp. 12, 18); typical of the aster family

follicle: a dry, pod-like fruit that splits open along a single line on 1 side (p. 150)

fringed: edged with a row of hairs (p. 151)

fruit: a ripened ovary, together with any other structures that develop with it as a unit

genus [genera]: a group of related plants or animals constituting a category of biological classification below family and above species; the first word of a scientific name indicates the genus, e.g., *Achillea* in *Achillea millefolium* (often abbreviated, e.g., *A. millefolium*)

gland: in plants, a small depression, bump or appendage that produces a thick, sticky or greasy fluid

glandular: with glands

herb: a plant that lacks woody above-ground parts and dies back to the ground in winter

COMPOUND-LEAF PARTS

palmately divided
(like fingers on a hand)

pinnately divided
(like barbs on a feather)

BLADE SHAPES

sword-like   slender
(linear)

oblong   lance-shaped

ovate   elliptic

oval   heart-shaped

FLOWER ARRANGEMENTS

spike   elongating cluster

umbrella-shaped cluster

FRUIT TYPES

achenes

schizocarp

drupe

capsule   follicle cluster

introduced: brought in from another region (e.g., from Europe), not native; such exotic plants often lack predators and other population controls present in the native range

keel: the two partly united lower petals of a pea-like flower (p. 152)

latex: milky plant juice containing rubbery compounds

leaflet: a single segment of a compound leaf (p. 149)

lens-shaped: discus-shaped, with 2 regular opposite sides either both curved or 1 curved and 1 flat (p. 150)

lip: a projection or expansion of a structure, such as the lower petal of a flower (p. 152)

lobe: a rounded or strap-shaped division of a leaf, petal or other structure (pp. 148, 151)

monoculture: a growth of only 1 kind of organism (e.g., 1 species of plant) in an area

mucilage: a sticky, gelatinous plant substance

mycorrhiza [mycorrhizae]: the mutually beneficial (symbiotic) association of certain fungi with the roots of certain seed plants

native: originating in a place (e.g., in Canada); indigenous

naturalized: originating in a distant region; introduced and growing wild in a new region

nerved: with prominent longitudinal lines or veins

noxious weed: an aggressive, usually introduced plant that rapidly invades sites where it is not wanted; in the legal sense, an invasive plant species requiring management or control because of legislative action

nutlet: a small, hard, dry, 1-seeded fruit or part of a fruit, not splitting open when mature

ovary: the structure at the base of a pistil that contains the young, undeveloped seeds (ovules) (p. 11)

palmate: divided into 3 or more lobes or leaflets that diverge from 1 point, like fingers on a hand (p. 149)

perennial: living for 3 or more years

persistent: remaining attached long after normal function has been completed

petal: a member of the inside ring of modified flower leaves, usually brightly coloured or white (pp. 11, 12)

pinnate: with parts (branches, lobes, leaflets, veins) arranged on both sides of a central stalk or vein, like the barbs of a feather; feather-like (p. 149)

pistil: the female organ of a flower, usually consisting of an ovary, style and stigma (p. 11)

pod: a dry fruit that splits open to release its seeds

pollen: the powdery contents of an anther, each grain containing male cells

pollinate: to transfer pollen from an anther to a stigma

pollination: the process of pollinating

prolific: producing many offspring

radially symmetrical: with parts arranged like spokes on a wheel, therefore divisible into equal parts along 2 or more lines (p. 19); compare 'bilaterally symmetrical'

rootstock: an underground, usually lengthened stem, distinguished from a true root by the presence of joints (nodes) and buds or scale-like leaves; a rhizome

rosette: a cluster of crowded, usually basal leaves in a circular arrangement (p. 148)

runner: a slender, horizontally spreading stem that often roots at its joints and tips

scale: any small, thin, flat structure

schizocarp: a dry fruit that splits into 2 or more parts when mature, e.g., fruits of the carrot family (p. 150)

sepal: a member of the outer ring of modified flower leaves, usually green and more or less leafy in texture but sometimes colourful (p. 11)

sheathing: partly or wholly surrounding another organ

simple: undivided (p. 148)

species (*abbrev.* **sp.**) [**species, spp.**]: a group of closely related plants or animals; the fundamental unit of biological classification, indicated by the second word of a scientific name (the specific epithet), e.g., *millefolium* in *Achillea millefolium*

specific epithet: see 'species'

spike: a simple, unbranched flower cluster, with (essentially) stalkless flowers arranged on an elongated main stalk (p. 150)

spindle-shaped: cylindrical and tapered to a point at both ends

spreading: diverging from the vertical, approaching horizontal

spur: a hollow appendage on a petal or sepal, usually functioning as a nectar gland (p. 152)

stamen: the pollen-bearing (male) organ of a flower, consisting of an anther and a filament (p. 11)

sterile: incapable of producing seed

stigma: the tip of the female organ (pistil), where the pollen lands (pp. 11, 12)

stipules: a pair of bract-like or leaf-like appendages at the base of a leaf stalk (p. 148)

strap-like floret: a small, often showy flower (floret) with a narrow, ribbon-like strap of fused petals, in a flowerhead of the aster family (p. 12); a ray floret

LEAF BLADE EDGES

wavy   rippled

toothed   sharp-toothed

spiny-toothed   fringed

finely   irregularly
blunt-toothed   coarse-toothed

shallowly lobed   deeply lobed

FLOWER SHAPES

tubular   funnel-shaped

bell-shaped   cupped

saucer-shaped

cross-shaped (4-petalled)

keel

wings

pea-like

upper lip

lower lip

spur

two-lipped

style: the part of the pistil connecting the stigma to the ovary, often elongated and stalk-like (pp. 11, 150)

subspecies (*abbrev.* subsp. *or* ssp.): a group of closely related plants or animals within a species, ranked below species and above variety in biological classification

taproot: a root system with a prominent main root, directed vertically downwards and bearing smaller side-roots, sometimes becoming very swollen and containing stored food material (starch or sugar), e.g., a carrot

tendril: a slender, clasping or twining outgrowth from a stem or leaf (p. 149)

tepal: a sepal or petal, when these structures are not easily distinguished

tooth: a small, often pointed lobe on the edge of a plant part (usually on a leaf) (pp. 148, 151)

trailing: spreading flat on the ground but not rooting

tuber: a thickened portion of a below-ground stem or root, serving for food storage and often also for propagation; e.g., a potato is a stem tuber

tubular floret: a small, tubular flower (floret) with fused petals, in a flowerhead of the aster family (p. 12); a disc floret

umbrella-shaped cluster: a branched flower grouping in which the branches radiate from 1 joint and curve upwards like the ribs of an umbrella to produce a flat-topped to rounded cluster (p. 150); an umbel

variety (*abbrev.* var.): a group of similar variants of a species, ranked below subspecies in biological classification

vegetative reproduction: producing new plants from asexual parts (e.g., rootstocks, leaves, stem fragments); the offspring so produced are genetically identical to (i.e., clones of) the parent plant

vein: a strand of conducting tubes (i.e., a vascular bundle containing phloem and xylem), especially if visible externally, as in a leaf (p. 148)

weed: a common, undesirable or troublesome plant that grows in abundance, especially on cultivated or waste ground; many of our weeds have been introduced from Eurasia; see also 'noxious weed'

whorl: a ring of 3 or more similar structures (e.g., leaves, branches or flowers) arising from 1 joint or node (p. 148)

wing: a thin, flattened expansion on the side(s) or tip of a plant part, e.g., on a seed or a stalk (p. 150); also, 1 of the 2 side-petals of a pea-like flower (p. 152)

winged: with 1 or more wings

winter-annual: a plant that grows from seed in late summer or fall, overwinters as a small plant and then flowers, fruits and dies the following spring or summer

Bubar, C. J., S. J. McColl et al. (2000). *Weeds of the Prairies*. Edmonton, Alberta Agriculture, Food and Rural Development.

Budd, A. C. (1957). *Wild Plants of the Canadian Prairies*. Ottawa, Canada Department of Agriculture.

Carmichael, L. T. (1961). *Prairie Wildflowers*. Toronto, J. M. Dent and Sons.

Coffey, T. (1993). *The History and Folklore of North American Wildflowers*. New York, Facts on File.

Cormack, R. G. H. (1977). *Wildflowers of Alberta*. Edmonton, Hurtig Publishers.

Couplan, F. (1998). *The Encyclopedia of Edible Plants of North America*. New Canaan, Keats Publishing.

Currah, R., A. Smreciu et al. (1983). *Prairie Wildflowers*. Edmonton, Friends of the Devonian Botanic Garden, University of Alberta.

Erichsen-Brown, C. (1979). *Use of Plants for the Past 500 Years*. Aurora, Breezy Creeks Press.

Foster, S. and J. A. Duke (1990). *Field Guide to Medicinal Plants: Eastern and Central North America*. Boston, Houghton Mifflin Company.

Grieve, M. (1931). *A Modern Herbal*. Harmondsworth, England, Jonathan Cape. Republished in 1976 by Penguin Books.

Johnson, D., L. Kershaw et al. (1995). *Plants of the Western Boreal Forest and Aspen Parkland*. Edmonton, Lone Pine Publishing.

Johnston, A. (1987). *Plants and the Blackfoot*. Lethbridge, Lethbridge Historical Society.

Kerik, J. and S. Fisher (1982). *Living with the Land: Use of Plants by the Native People of Alberta*. Edmonton, Provincial Museum of Alberta.

Kershaw, L. (2000). *Edible and Medicinal Plants of the Rockies*. Edmonton, Lone Pine Publishing.

Looman, J. and K. F. Best (1979). *Budd's Flora of the Canadian Prairie Provinces*. Hull, Canadian Government Publishing Centre.

Marles, R. L., C. Clavelle et al. (2000). *Aboriginal Plant Use in Canada's Northwest Boreal Forest*. Vancouver, UBC Press.

Moss, E. H. (1983). *Flora of Alberta*. 2nd edition. Revised by J. G. Packer. Toronto, University of Toronto Press.

Mulligan, G. A. and D. B. Munro (1990). *Poisonous Plants of Canada*. Ottawa, Agriculture Canada.

Peirce, A. (1999). *The American Pharmaceutical Association Practical Guide to Natural Medicines*. New York, William Morrow and Company.

Reader's Digest (1986). *Magic and Medicine of Plants*. Montreal, The Reader's Digest Association.

Robinson, P. (1979). *Profiles of Northwest Plants: Food Uses, Medicinal Uses, Legends*. Portland, Far West Book Service.

Royer, F. and R. Dickinson (1998). *Weeds of Canada and the Northern United States: A Guide for Identification*. Edmonton, University of Alberta Press.

Schofield, J. J. (1989). *Discovering Wild Plants: Alaska, Western Canada, the Northwest*. Anchorage, Alaska Northwest Books.

Stokes, D. and L. Stokes (1985). *A Guide to Enjoying Wildflowers*. Toronto, Little, Brown and Company.

Tilford, G. L. (1997). *Edible and Medicinal Plants of the West*. Missoula, Mountain Press Publishing Company.

Vance, F. R., J. R. Jowsey et al. (1977). *Wildflowers Across the Prairies*. Saskatoon, Western Producer Prairie Books.

Wilkinson, K. (1999). *Wildflowers of Alberta*. Edmonton, University of Alberta Press and Lone Pine Publishing.

Willard, T. (1992). *Edible and Medicinal Plants of the Rocky Mountains and Neighbouring Territories*. Calgary, Wild Rose College of Natural Healing.

Common Name	Scientific Name	Page Numbers
Arum Family	Araceae	61
Aster Family	Asteraceae	64–93
Bellflower Family	Campanulaceae	146
Bladderwort Family	Lentibulariaceae	40
Borage Family	Boraginaceae	143–145
Buck-bean Family	Menyanthaceae	108
Buttercup Family	Ranunculaceae	44, 116–120
Cactus Family	Cactaceae	114
Carrot Family	Apiaceae	95–98
Dogbane Family	Apocynaceae	142
Dogwood Family	Cornaceae	62
Evening-primrose Family	Onagraceae	139–140
Figwort Family	Scrophulariaceae	38–39, 100, 141
Flax Family	Linaceae	137
Fumitory Family	Fumariaceae	37
Geranium Family	Geraniaceae	136
Goosefoot Family	Chenopodiaceae	63
Heath Family	Ericaceae	135
Iris Family	Iridaceae	110
Lily Family	Liliaceae	111–113
Madder Family	Rubiaceae	103
Mallow Family	Malvaceae	138
Mint Family	Lamiaceae	41–43, 101–102
Morning-glory Family	Convolvulaceae	147
Mustard Family	Brassicaceae	105–107
Orchid Family	Orchidaceae	36
Pea Family	Fabaceae	47–59
Pink Family	Caryophyllaceae	122–123
Primrose Family	Primulaceae	124–125
Rose Family	Rosaceae	126–134
Sandalwood Family	Santalaceae	99
Saxifrage Family	Saxifragaceae	121
Smartweed Family	Polygonaceae	60, 104
Spurge Family	Euphorbiaceae	94
Violet Family	Violaceae	45–46
Water-lily Family	Nymphaeaceae	115
Water-plantain Family	Alismataceae	109

- ☐ Alexanders, heart-leaved
- ☐ alfalfa
- ☐ American-aster, fringed
- ☐ American-aster, smooth blue
- ☐ anemone, Canada
- ☐ arrowhead, arum-leaved
- ☐ avens, three-flowered
- ☐ avens, yellow
- ☐ beardtongue, slender blue
- ☐ bedstraw, northern
- ☐ bergamot, wild
- ☐ bindweed, field
- ☐ bird's-foot-trefoil
- ☐ bladderwort, greater
- ☐ blanketflower, great
- ☐ bluebells, tall
- ☐ blue-eyed-grass, common
- ☐ buck-bean
- ☐ bunchberry
- ☐ burdock, woolly
- ☐ butter-and-eggs
- ☐ buttercup, meadow
- ☐ cactus, prickly-pear
- ☐ calla, water
- ☐ campion, bladder
- ☐ chamomile, scentless
- ☐ cinquefoil, graceful
- ☐ cinquefoil, plains
- ☐ cinquefoil, shrubby
- ☐ clover, alsike
- ☐ clover, red
- ☐ coneflower, prairie
- ☐ corydalis, golden
- ☐ cow-parsnip, common
- ☐ crane's-bill, northern
- ☐ daisy, oxeye
- ☐ dandelion, common
- ☐ death-camas, white
- ☐ dock, curly
- ☐ dogbane, spreading
- ☐ evening-primrose, common
- ☐ false-dandelion, pale
- ☐ false-golden-aster, hairy
- ☐ false-Solomon's-seal, starry
- ☐ false-toadflax
- ☐ fireweed, common
- ☐ flax, wild blue
- ☐ fleabane, Philadelphia
- ☐ fleabane, smooth
- ☐ giant-hyssop, blue
- ☐ globe-mallow, scarlet
- ☐ goat's-beard, common
- ☐ golden-bean
- ☐ goldenrod, Canada
- ☐ goldenrod, spike-like
- ☐ grass-of-Parnassus, northern
- ☐ gromwell, fringed
- ☐ gumweed, curly-cup
- ☐ harebell
- ☐ hawk's-beard, annual
- ☐ hawkweed, narrow-leaved
- ☐ hedge-nettle, hairy
- ☐ hemp-nettle, brittle-stem
- ☐ knapweed, spotted
- ☐ Labrador-tea, rusty
- ☐ lady's-slipper, yellow
- ☐ larkspur, tower
- ☐ lettuce, common blue
- ☐ licorice, American
- ☐ lily, wood
- ☐ locoweed, showy
- ☐ marsh-marigold, yellow
- ☐ milk-vetch, American
- ☐ mint, wild
- ☐ mountain-avens, yellow
- ☐ mouse-ear-chickweed, field
- ☐ mullein, great
- ☐ mustard, tumbleweed
- ☐ mustard, wild
- ☐ paintbrush, common red
- ☐ pineappleweed
- ☐ pond-lily, yellow
- ☐ prairie-crocus
- ☐ pussytoes, rosy
- ☐ ragwort, marsh
- ☐ rose, prickly
- ☐ shootingstar, saline
- ☐ silverweed, common
- ☐ smartweed, water
- ☐ sow-thistle, perennial
- ☐ spurge, leafy
- ☐ strawberry, Virginia
- ☐ strawberry-blite
- ☐ sunflower, annual
- ☐ sweet-clover
- ☐ sweet-colt's-foot, arctic
- ☐ sweet-vetch, American
- ☐ tansy, common
- ☐ thistle, Canada
- ☐ vetch, American
- ☐ vetch, bird
- ☐ vetchling, cream-coloured
- ☐ violet, Canada
- ☐ violet, early blue
- ☐ viper's-bugloss, common
- ☐ wallflower, wormseed
- ☐ watercrowfoot, yellow
- ☐ water-hemlock, spotted
- ☐ water-parsnip, common
- ☐ wood-aster, showy
- ☐ yarrow, common
- ☐ yellow-loosestrife, fringed

*A*n avid naturalist since childhood, Linda Kershaw focused on botany at the University of Waterloo, earning her master's degree in 1976. Since then she has worked as a consultant and researcher in northwestern Canada and as an author and editor in Edmonton, while pursuing two favourite pastimes—photography and illustrating. Linda hopes that her books will help people appreciate the beauty and fascinating history of plants and recognize the intrinsic value of nature's rich mosaic. Linda is the author or co-author of 10 Lone Pine field guides, including *Plants of the Western Boreal Forest and Aspen Parkland.*

Over many years in the field with Linda, sons Geoff (left, 16 field seasons) and Eric (21 seasons) and husband Peter (far right, 29 seasons) have travelled thousands of kilometres and developed sharp eyes in the never-ending search for wild plants and animals. They've also learned the virtue of patience as 15-minute walks turn into 2-hour photo sessions. Linda dedicates the wayside wildflower guides to her family, to thank them for their continued patience and support and for many happy hours of hiking through wild and not-so-wild places.